Succeeding From the Margins of Canadian Society

A Strategic Resource for New Immigrants, Refugees and International Students

by

Francis Adu-Febiri, PhD
and Everett Ofori, MBA

CCB Publishing
British Columbia, Canada

Succeeding From the Margins of Canadian Society: A Strategic Resource for New Immigrants, Refugees and International Students

Copyright ©2009 by Francis Adu-Febiri and Everett Ofori
ISBN-13 978-1-926585-27-7
First Edition

Library and Archives Canada Cataloguing in Publication
Adu-Febiri, Francis, 1956-
Succeeding from the margins of Canadian society: a strategic resource for new immigrants, refugees and international students / written by Francis Adu-Febiri and Everett Ofori – 1st ed.
Includes bibliographical references and index.
ISBN 978-1-926585-27-7
Also available in electronic format.
1. Minorities--Employment--Canada. 2. Immigrants--Employment--Canada.
3. Refugees--Employment--Canada. 4. Students, Foreign--Employment--Canada.
5. Minorities--Canada--Economic conditions--21st century.
6. Immigrants--Canada--Economic conditions--21st century.
7. Refugees--Canada--Economic conditions--21st century.
8. Students, Foreign--Canada--Economic conditions--21st century.
9. Canada--Emigration and immigration--Economic aspects. 10. Multiculturalism--Canada.
11. Affirmative action programs--Canada. 12. Canada--Social conditions--1991-.
I. Ofori, Everett, 1963- II. Title.
FC104.A38 2009   305.800971   C2009-903084-5

Publisher: CCB Publishing
             British Columbia, Canada
             www.ccbpublishing.com

*To Ernestina Adu-Febiri of Victoria, Ellen H. Reynolds of Toronto
and all immigrants, refugees and international students.*

CONTENTS

PREFACE

Books about racial and cultural minorities in Canada tend to focus on barriers, injustices, inequalities, rejections, and frustrations that marginalize these categories of people in Canada. What is often neglected is the fact that many minorities succeed in Canada from the margins of Canadian society. This book contributes to filling this gap by documenting 1) minority successes in the face of systemic marginalization, 2) the strategic resources that work for these minorities, and 3) lessons new immigrants, refugees and international students can learn from these success stories.

The Canadian social structure, like any social structure in contemporary human society, creates and supports unequal opportunity structures. A major dimension of the inequality is against racial and ethnic minority immigrants, refugees and international students. Social inequality tends to block or limit socio-economic mobility of these minoritized peoples. Critical intellectuals and social activists highlight this characteristic of Canadian society, creating the impression that this unequal social structure is a crack-free glass ceiling for minorities. It is the stance of this book that since many racial and ethnic minorities in Canada have succeeded in business, education, politics, and the professions, the Canadian social structure is not crack-free. There are cracks in unequal societies that many minorities have utilized as escape routes to facilitate their social mobility. The wedges these minorities use to widen the cracks for their upward mobility include strategic resources such as appropriate knowledge, relevant skills, abilities, facilities, strategic planning and decisions, mentoring, networking opportunities, and family and community support systems. These strategic resources are the secrets behind the hard work, ingenious application of intelligence, and personal ambitions of successful minorities in Canada. New immigrants, refugees and international students in Canada who become aware of these wedges and are motivated to utilize them would experience social mobility. As more and more minorities move through these cracks, a critical mass of minority business people, politicians, and professionals would form to become a power base to successfully strategize and negotiate for the transformation of the unequal Canadian social structure. The legendary *Underground Railway* is a relevant analogy for this standpoint of the book. Slavery in America was a big inequality structure that trapped the lives of Blacks. However, there were always cracks in the American slave society and some of the slaves developed wedges and used them to widen the cracks for their escape. One of the major widened cracks was the *Underground Railway* that became a prominent escape route for American slaves to freedom in Canada. As more and more slaves escaped through the cracks, a critical mass of free slaves was formed to initiate the civil rights movement that provided constitutional rights for Blacks in America and Canada. The main secret behind the success of the *Underground Railway* was that the slaves received strategic resources such as support network, food, money, compasses, and protective weapons.

This book although does not get into the theories of inequality, equity and diversity, it does acknowledge the structural and cultural barriers to minority success in Canada. That is, it does not blame the failure of individual minorities to make it in Canada on their lack of hard work, individual intelligence and personal ambition. Rather, like the *Underground Railway* escape network, it points to strategic resources that new immigrants, refugees and international students can use to help them overcome some of the barriers to success in Canada. With the right and adequate resources, new immigrants, refugees and international students could effectively connect with Canadian society and Canadian academia to facilitate their upward social mobility. Part I of the book addresses minority struggles, successes, and prospects for connecting to the mainstream Canadian society. In Part II the strategic resources that minorities could utilize to successfully connect to the Canadian education system are provided. The main theme running through both parts is that new immigrants, refugees and international students in Canada, although are structurally located in the margins of Canadian society, they can succeed in the mainstream society from these margins when they are connected to strategic resources.

In the context of the book, Immigrants, Refugees and International Students are operationally defined. Immigrants refer to people formally coming to Canada from other countries as settlers. On the other hand, Refugees are people who do not enter Canada through the formal processes of immigration. They come from other countries to seek refuge in Canada because of political, economic, and cultural problems they experience in their countries, and Canadians who seek refuge in post-secondary education because of employment problems. The concept of international students is used to represent Students from countries outside Canada and the United States.

To put the book in a personal context, the following introduces the authors. Francis Adu-Febiri and Everett Ofori were both born and raised in Ghana, West Africa. Both went through the Ghanaian school system before coming to Canada.

Francis Adu-Febiri came to Canada as an international (graduate) student. He later immigrated and became a Canadian citizen. He received his Master's Degree in Sociology from Simon Fraser University and a PhD from the University of British Columbia. Dr. Adu-Febiri is currently Sociology Professor in the Department of Social Sciences at Camosun College, British Columbia, Canada. He was the Chair of the Department from June 2002 to May 2005. He is also an Associate of the Faculty of Graduate Studies at the University of Victoria, Canada, and an Adjunct Professor in the Faculty of Education at Simon Fraser University, Canada. He has taught as a term faculty at Simon Fraser University, the University of British Columbia and the University of Victoria. He has also supervised a Master's thesis at Royal Roads

University in Victoria. Francis has presented and published extensively on tourism, human factor development, globalization, diversity, racialization, and ethnicity. He is the author of *First Nations Students Talk Back: Voices of a Learning People*. Dr. Adu-Febiri is the founder and president of Workplace Diversity Consulting Services (WDCS), and serves as the Chair of the Ethnocultural Advisory Committee of the Ministry of Children and Family Development, Victoria, British Columbia. He has been the president of the Canadian Chapter of the International Institute for Human Factor Development (IIHFD) since 2000.

Everett Ofori, a Ghanaian-born Canadian writer, has lived in Quebec, Ontario, and British Columbia. He is the author of *Prepare for Greatness: How to Make Your Success Inevitable* and *The Changing Japanese Woman: From Yamatonadeshiko to Yamatonadegucci (English/Japanese)*. He worked in the early 1990s as an assistant editor for the Vancouver-based publication *Common Ground*. In addition to four years of volunteer service as an English teacher with the Intercultural Association of Greater Victoria (British Columbia), Everett has coached hundreds of university and high school students both in Canada and Asia on how to hone their oral and written communication skills. He holds a Master's in Business Administration (MBA) degree from Heriot-Watt University (Scotland) and is now about half-way through his Doctorate program.

Francis Adu-Febiri and Everett Ofori
May 2009

ACKNOWLEDGMENTS

We would like to take this opportunity to acknowledge the help and support we received from various sources in completing this book. Our greatest thank you goes to Paul Rabinovitch of CCB Publishing. Paul had the foresight to see the potential of the manuscript and encouraged us to refine it for publication. He also insisted that we get permission from publishers for the numerous quotations and paraphrases we have used to support our arguments in the manuscript. His editorial comments were a very useful guide in revising the manuscript.

To all the publishers in Canada and the United States who granted us permission to use quotations and paraphrases from their published works, we say a big thank you to you.

We are grateful to Margaret Matthews of Vancouver for allowing us to use her *Chocolate in a Vanilla World* story to enrich the introduction of the book.

Our sincere gratitude goes to all the racial and ethnic minorities in Canada whose painful struggles and spectacular successes inspired us to consider writing this book.

We also acknowledge the moral support of Mrs. Ernestina Adu-Febiri of Victoria, Mrs. Ellen H. Reynolds of Toronto, Professor Renee Warburton of the University of Victoria, Professor Senyo Adjibolosoo of Point Loma Nazarene University in San Diego, Professor Joseph Mensah of York University, and Professor Francis Yee of Camosun College in Victoria.

INTRODUCTION

RACIAL/ETHNIC MINORITIES IN CANADIAN SOCIETY: CONSTRAINTS, SUCCESSES AND POSSIBILITIES

There are cracks in the barriers to minority success in Canada that can be opened up to facilitate the socio-economic mobility of racial/ethnic minorities. It takes strategic resources such as appropriate information and knowledge, relevant skills, mentoring, networking opportunities, and family/community support to open up these cracks to utilize existing opportunity structures in Canada. Hard work, individual intelligence and personal ambition play a very small role. Despite Canada's multiculturalism policy, new immigrants, refugees and international students in Canada cannot succeed without having the right and adequate resources to connect to the opportunity structures in the mainstream Canadian culture.

Many immigrants, refugees, and international students have come to Canada with the belief that the hard work, intelligence, ambition, tenacity, maturity, and other personal qualities that made them successful in their old countries and helped them survive what might have been a treacherous journey would also help them to succeed in Canada. Unfortunately, this has not always been the case. Such overconfidence has been the undoing of many an immigrant, refugee and international student. Far too many have been blindsided in the benign looking environment of Canada, forcing them to abandon their dreams and to accept conditions of life that they would never have imagined a few years before. Not taking the time to understand the Canadian system, the underlying rules that govern life, and strategic resources that facilitate success can be pricey in the long run. Taking the time to find out the available strategic resources and how to effectively utilize them will save you from the kind of mistakes that have sidelined many immigrants, refugees and international students and turned them into bitter wrecks with nothing good to say about Canada. The point is that it takes strategic resources to enhance one's hard work, intelligence, talents, abilities and ambition to make the stories about Canada as land of milk and honey a reality.

Although Canada claims to be a multicultural country, the reality is that conventional rewards are located in the upper/middle class Anglo and Franco cultures of both the larger society and academia. Those who have access to strategic resources to effectively connect with the opportunity structures of the mainstream culture and/or academia are those who get most conventional rewards. New entrants to Canada who remain disconnected from strategic resources remain secluded in their minority cultures and tend to experience trapped socio-economic mobility. Real life experiences of immigrants, refugees and international students support this claim. The fact is connecting with the opportunity structures in the mainstream Canadian culture and academia from a culture on the margins requires appropriate information and knowledge, definitive decisions on the choices the information presents, mentoring, relevant networking, and a strong support system. Unless they have many of these strategic resources, immigrants, refugees and international students cannot fully participate in the mainstream Canadian society. And unless they can participate fully in the mainstream culture, success in Canada is likely to elude them. They would be unable to realize their talents, obtain higher education, get well-paying jobs or create and sustain viable economic enterprises.

For new immigrants, refugees, and international students, basic skills are not enough because of the reality that unequal opportunity structures exist in Canadian society and academia that tend to work against minorities because of racism, ethnocentrism and other social injustices embedded in the Canadian social structure. Therefore racial and ethnic minorities are located in the margins of Canadian society and their success may not be determined by hard work, individual intelligence and personal ambition. Should new immigrants, refugees and international students despair and lose faith in themselves because of racism, ethnocentrism and injustices in Canadian society and academia? No! There is a way out! Many immigrants, refugees and international students have proven that there is some wisdom in the popular notion in the minority communities that says because of racism and ethnocentrism in Canada minorities need higher than average qualifications, abilities, skills, mentors, and support systems in order to achieve success. This book introduces new immigrants, refugees and international students to strategic resources that successful racial and cultural minorities have used to acquire and utilize the extra qualifications, knowledge, skills, abilities, networking and support systems to go beyond the ordinary to experience extraordinary success in Canadian society. The reality is that new immigrants, refugees and international students can succeed in Canadian society and academia despite the prevalence of racism, ethnocentrism and other barriers they face. *Chocolate can thrive in a Vanilla World!*

BEING *CHOCOLATE* IN A *VANILLA* WORLD: THE STORY OF MARGARET MATTHEWS

Prior to my migrating to Canada from a predominantly non-White country, several "well meaning" Seniors gave me unsolicited advice that I was making a big mistake in migrating to a White country, where I would be a victim of racial prejudice and discrimination; that I would not have a chance of ever getting married since I was a Black female. Their rationalizing was that a White male would not want me, neither would a Black male (since Black males seem to want White females, either because of self-hatred or an inferiority complex about being Black) and that generally speaking, I would be very unhappy and probably die an "Old Maid" in isolation. What words of comfort for a high-spirited young lady! Incidentally, these "well-meaning friends" had never been to North America, and did not have much first-hand knowledge about life in Canada. They had only heard about Blacks being in slavery to their White masters and their inhumane treatment of them. They had also read in U.S. magazines about Lena Horne, Sammy Davis, Jr. and other Black celebrities who had been denied service at restaurants, and refused a hotel room in classy hotels.

After weighing the pros and cons, I made my decision to take the plunge and face up to the challenges that came my way. I would make the best of the situation, and brush off any racial slurs, discrimination and anti-social behaviour towards me as water off a duck's back.

During my first year in Canada, I did run into some subtle forms of discrimination, but chose not to let it bother me. If some Whites did not want to associate or socialize with me because of my race or colour, that was their problem. I had no time for them in my life either, for I had better things to do. However, I was curious about Black history and Black culture and read extensively about the subject. I borrowed the book *Uncle Tom's Cabin* from the public library and was astounded at the inhumane treatment of the slaves by their White masters who were plantation owners. I was determined to learn more about the subject, and so read every book and article that I could lay my hands on. I was fascinated with Martin Luther King, Jr.'s *"I Have a Dream"*, the Civil Rights Movement, and his non-violent strategies to attain his dream. Although he did not live long enough to see his dream become a reality, he left a legacy that will remain in the echelons of Black history indefinitely. Malcolm X had a more aggressive strategy to achieve his goals, and met a martyr's death. The writings of other Black civil rights activists captivated me, as a whole new world opened up before me. A book that particularly intrigued me was entitled *Black Like Me* which was the experience of a White man in the U.S. who dyed the skin of his entire body with jet-black ink, wore an Afro wig and went to live in the southern states posing as a Black male. He defiantly went into the "Whites Only" restaurants, hotels and other public places to see how the White population would treat him as a Black male. He met with the same negative treatment and discrimination as a Black, and after about six months to a year of his experiment, went back to his home, took off his disguise and wrote the aforesaid book. An incredible story of racial hatred and discrimination against Blacks!

Some years ago a television series *"Roots"* was aired on NBC for several days and I did not miss a single one of the airings. The inhumane treatment of the slaves captured and brought from Africa on the slave-ships appalled me. Later when they arrived in the United States and were bought on the auction block by the plantation owners to work as slaves brought tears to my eyes. Kunta Kinte, the runaway slave's escape to freedom was short-lived, as his White master who pursued and captured him cut off his foot so he could not run away again. *Man's inhumanity to man!* The sexual harassment of the White plantation owners towards their Black female slaves and their illegitimate children (born out of wedlock) shocked and astounded me.

About this time in my sojourns in Canada there was an influx of "visible minorities" from various parts of the world who arrived as immigrants, and the *Multicultural Act* was passed. Canada has accepted immigrants from various parts of the world and has treated them with respect and dignity. Racial discrimination was going out the window gradually as "visible minorities" were dating and inter-marrying Whites. During this time I was asked to go out on dates by White men. One Swiss guy in particular, who saw me at a social event, took a fancy to me from the start. He came over and got acquainted, which resulted in a long steady relationship. It turned out that although he was White, he was *only attracted to Black females, and all his previous girlfriends were Black females.* I chuckled when he told me this. I took photos of myself and my Swiss boyfriend and sent them back home to my friends who were amazed that I had broken the ice and defied tradition.

Recently I have taken a course in Women's Studies and Gender Relations. I learned about the anger of women of colour directed towards White women and the system that put the latter in the center and the former in the margins of society. It can, however, be argued that there are a few prominent women of colour who, having faced the challenges of abuse, poverty and discrimination, have overcome these obstacles and risen to national recognition. For example, at the late Rosa Parks' funeral, Oprah Winfrey gave the eulogy that was televised on national television. Her comments were that but for Rosa Parks' refusal to stand in that bus and give her seat to a White person, she would not be standing there today on Capitol Hill, among Heads of States and other dignitaries. Rosa was willing to go to prison for a just cause.

Another such prominent Black female is the present Governor General of Canada, Michaëlle Jean who immigrated to Canada with her parents as a young girl of eleven as poor, Black immigrants from Haiti. However, through hard work, perseverance, the right family and community support systems, she overcame those challenges, obtained a University education, worked for the Canadian Broadcasting Corporation (CBC) as a bilingual television-journalist, and eventually was appointed, and serves faithfully as the Governor General of Canada.

Yet another Black female of national prominence is Condoleezza Rice, former Secretary of State in the Bush administration who also had to fight racism, sexism and other forms of discrimination. Her doctoral degree that she earned secured her a prominent position in politics, and recently it has been suggested that she run for President of the United States. One wonders whether the United States is ready for a Black *Female* President at this time in its history, however, that is left to be seen.

Perhaps the role model of many a Black female, including myself, is Oprah Winfrey. Her autobiography reveals her many struggles ever since her birth as an illegitimate child, abandoned and abused in the Deep South, her survival and rise to fame, fortune and national recognition as a living symbol of hope and success. At the age of ten, she sat on her kitchen floor in the Deep South and watched Sidney Poitier on television receive an Oscar, and determined that if a Black Male could receive an Oscar, there was hope that some day she might too. Her dreams came true when she grew up and received innumerable Emmys and awards for her many roles in films and other contributions to society. As a Black woman in a business that is dominated by White males, she has made it to the top with remarkable determination and talent, and her assets as a billionaire makes her one of the richest and most popular Black females in the United States today. Amazing business acumen!

While Audre Lorde and other Black Feminists focus on inequality and injustice towards Women of Colour, Winfrey emphasizes her consciousness about her legacy as a Black person more so than many Blacks. However, unlike a lot of Black people who are very angry and bitter, she won't be angry and bitter. Oprah is proud of her Black heritage, a fact usually reflected in her films and television programs as well as in her many public appearances and speeches. Winfrey is world renowned, as she is read, heard, watched on television and admired around the world.

Does a Black female have to despair and lose faith in herself because of the social injustices prevalent around her? Should she not be motivated and ambitious to strive for success to get ahead in life and fulfill her dreams and ambitions? The above Black women have proven to the world that the barriers of Racism, Sexism and Classism can be shattered and trodden over, and one can reach the pinnacles of success through diligence, determination, and family/community support. The sky is the limit for those who dare to follow their dreams, regardless of whether you are *chocolate* or *vanilla*.

* * * * *

The point is that there are always cracks in structural barriers of human society, and it takes the right and adequate resources to open them up for individual success. Many immigrants, refugees and international students enter Canada uninformed about the real barriers to their success in this country. The economic, political, social and cultural problems that these racial and cultural minorities encounter from Canadian institutions, organizations, communities and individuals overwhelm and break many of them. However, some of them break records in the face of the frustrations they encounter. What accounts for the success of the latter group of immigrants, refugees and international students in Canada? Using the secrets that facilitated the successes of these minorities as templates and also the observations on how the Canadian society and the education system operate, this book suggests strategic resources that would facilitate minority connections to Canadian mainstream institutions and organizations to win from the margins of society. Failure to connect strategically spells trapped socio-economic mobility and/or school dropout for minorities, and many minorities have fallen into this trap for lack of appropriate information and knowledge of the workings of Canadian society, relevant skills to confront these barriers as much as lack of adequate mentoring and support networks to help overcome the structural barriers.

Some immigrants, refugees and international students have effectively avoided or transcended the exclusion and assimilation traps to achieve remarkable successes in Canada by strategic connections to Canadian mainstream society and education system. This provides a solid foundation for the stance of this book that new immigrants, refugees and international students do not have to settle for underachievement despite the cultural and structural disadvantages they face in Canada. The strategic resources the book provides serve as an important conduit to help these racial and cultural minorities to productively connect with Canadian society and/or academia from the margins.

This book does not get into the theories of inequality, equity and diversity because new immigrants, refugees and international students are more interested in practical resources that would help them negotiate structural and cultural minefields of Canadian society and academia. The book, however, acknowledges the structural and cultural barriers to minority success in Canada. That is, it does not blame individual minorities for not making it in Canada. Organizationally the book is composed of two sections: 1) Connecting with Canadian society and 2) Connecting with Canadian academia.

Part I plunges into the contested issue of problematizing Canada as the best place on earth to live. Although Canada claims to be a multicultural country, the reality is that conventional rewards are located in the upper/middle class Anglo and Franco institutions and organizations of both the larger society and the standards of mainstream academia. These institutions and organizations tend to relegate racial and cultural minorities into the margins of Canadian society. Those minorities who successfully connect with the mainstream from the margins are those who get conventional rewards, thus winning from the margins. New entrants to Canada who remain isolated in the margins of the Canadian public sphere tend to experience low or no socio-economic mobility. Connecting from the margins is a process that requires strategic resources. Real life experiences of immigrants, refugees and international students supporting these claims form the basis of the discussions in Chapters One through Ten.

In Part II, it is argued that Canadian academia espouses standards, requirements and expectations that differ very much from those of the countries and communities that produce the greater majority of immigrants, refugees, international students, and indigenous people for Canada. Most immigrants, refugees and international students who enter the school system therefore experience academic culture shock. To succeed in the Canadian education system they need to overcome this culture shock to effectively connect with the Canadian academic culture. This academic culture projects the ideals of critical or analytical thinking, Greco-Roman logical reasoning and communication system, problem identification, and problem solving. This section proposes that in order to meet these academic cultural goals, immigrants, refugees and international students new to the education system need to acquire and apply the Canadian standards and expectations in the crucial areas of knowledge and skills such as structured listening, critical thinking and reading, academic writing, class participation, effective note taking/making, doing research and presentations, and taking examinations. Chapters Eleven through Twenty Five provide guides and tips for mastering these vital knowledge and skills that may help students to excel in the Canadian education system despite the fact that curriculum and pedagogy tend to marginalize their experiences and histories.

The concluding chapter tackles the controversial issue of connecting or integrating into Canadian mainstream society and academia without assimilating. It argues that until the multiculturalism and anti-racism projects eliminate monoculturalism and monostructuralism from Canada, strategic connections of minorities with mainstream institutions, organizations and communities from the margins would be the key to their success in Canadian society. That is, under these constraints minorities can only win from the margins. It is feasible for minorities to connect with the mainstream without being absorbed by it. Immigrants, refugees and international students can acquire the norms, knowledge, skills, standards, expectations, and images of the Canadian mainstream without giving up their ethnic-specific values, beliefs and identities. Some racial and cultural minorities have successfully done this.

There is hope for new immigrants, refugees and international students in Canada who want to succeed. They can successfully connect to the mainstream society and academia from the margins without assimilating.

PART I

CONNECTING TO THE MAINSTREAM CANADIAN SOCIETY

Culture is made up of values, beliefs, norms, symbols, expectations, arts and crafts, technology, and other ways of life. Most immigrants, refugees and international students would have no trouble adapting to the Canadian ideal values because these are values that most freedom loving people cherish. These include fairness, tolerance, respect, honesty, accountability, integrity, openness, diversity, cooperation, democracy, equal opportunity, and civil and environmental responsibility. Although Christianity is the main belief system of Canada, the country has several other religions: Islam, Hinduism, Buddhism, Sikhism, Judaism, and Animism. Many other Canadians are not affiliated with any conventional form of religion. Because of the operation of diversity of religions in Canadian society, new entrants to society, whatever their religions would find a place or community of worshipers. In the areas of dressing and technology, because of globalization (westernization?), many immigrants, refugees and international students easily adjust to Canadian standards. Perhaps the most difficult aspects of Canadian culture for new entrants, particularly adults, to adapt to are English/French expressions and accent, body language, jokes, and foods.

Generally, then, the adaptation of new immigrants, refugees and international students to the Canadian ideal culture should not be too hard. It would be inaccurate and naïve, however, to assume that mainstream Canadians apply these cultural elements in their real everyday lives. Rather, if you approach these cultural values and beliefs as just ideals towards which Canadians are continually aspiring, you will be less shocked when you encounter the entrenched and widespread instances of intolerance, disrespect, and/or injustice from people or institutions that you expected would epitomize these fine values and beliefs.

CHAPTER ONE

OH! CANADA

Canada Welcomes You

Each year, Canada welcomes people from over one hundred and fifty countries. All these people live together in harmony while pursuing their individual goals and sharing in the improvement of their local communities and the country as a whole. New Canadians, regardless of their backgrounds, come bearing their own gifts and talents and perspectives, all of which contribute to the growth and continued prosperity of the country. Canadian leaders recognize the contributions that immigrants have made over the years and acknowledge that for the country to remain prosperous the knowledge, skills, talents, and hard work of immigrants are needed. For immigrants to feel at home, however, it has been necessary, from time to time, for the government to step in where the expectations for the exercise of goodwill and decency on the part of ordinary Canadians may have fallen short. Immigrants have also occasionally had to appraise their ways of doing things and to show sensitivity to their neighbours, friends and fellow Canadians. Yes, Canada is committed to equality, and new entrants are certain to experience, sooner or later, some of the sense of caring and concern that Canadians show for one another. Indeed, as a new immigrant you can look upon other Canadians as fellow workers in the crafting and shaping of a society that moves ever closer towards the ideals of fairness, justice, and equality for all.

So committed is Canada to fairness that the idea of equality has been included in the *Canadian Charter of Rights and Freedoms*. Equal but separate, however, is not the notion here. As the Citizenship and Immigration Canada publication *A Look at Canada* points out, "In Canada, we also believe in the importance of working together and helping one another." Anyone who comes with the full willingness to help make Canada work for all is likely to find in Canada's system the opportunity to also reach personal goals while contributing to an ideal that has made Canada the frequent recipient of the United Nations' honour of being the best country in the world in which to live.

Canada Needs You

The Canadian government, with all kinds of statistics at its disposal, is all too aware of the need to prepare the country against possible skills shortages. The projected shortages range from medical technicians and construction tradesmen to university professors, of which the need is projected in the tens of thousands. Nurses, who are apparently already in short supply, are going to be in even greater demand over the years. But already, immigrants in Canada have proven their worth. They make up a large proportion of the labour force and are a major driving force of economic growth in Canada. The match between immigrants and Canada would seem to be a perfect one, with immigrants helping to shore up the economy and Canada giving them a safe environment in which to raise their families. In fact, other than First Nations people all Canadians can trace their history to immigration, two, three, or maybe even seven generations back. In a very real sense then, Canada has been built on immigration, a tradition that has also garnered the country much international respect. The room Canadians give one another and the tolerance they show for one another is increasingly seen as a model for the rest of the world.

Canada, one of the most peaceful, progressive, and prosperous nations in the world, is a magnet for people from all over the world. The name 'Canada' is like a talisman that promises protection from persecution and privation. It is like an amulet that promises to ward off the twin evils of poverty and hopelessness. Immigrants come with the full awareness that in order for them to achieve their goals they have to work hard. Yes, hard work is necessary but it is not sufficient to achieve the Canadian dream. In addition to hard work, the new immigrant, refugee or international student needs to be connected with strategic resources such as community, relevant Canadian educational credentials, and/or intimate knowledge of employment or business opportunities in Canadian society. It was so when Chinese labourers helped build railway lines in Canada in the late 19th century and it is so as new streams of immigrants come in from Africa, Latin America, and Eastern Europe. One such individual for whom the Canadian dream has come true is James Chim who came to Canada over 30 years ago from Hong Kong and began his life in Canada as an MBA student at the University of Saskatchewan. After working for seventeen years at the Canadian Imperial Bank of Commerce he struck out on his own and opened a chain of Japanese restaurants in the United States. Sarku Japan, of which Mr. Chim is the president and CEO, is headquartered in Markham, Ontario, and has over 170 outlets, mostly in malls and shopping centres. James Chim and other successful international students and immigrants help fuel the dream that Canada is indeed a land of opportunity and possibilities. Canada needs you; if you stay long enough and do your part for Canada and your fellow Canadians you might even begin to feel, more than just being needed, you are wanted.

Stranger in a New Land

It takes a certain measure of courage for one to abandon the comfort of hearth and home, one's community, one's country, one's home and native land, to settle elsewhere. But migrating from one place to another is a common human response in

4

the face of economic, social, political, or other challenges. It is by no means the only response but it is one that is not usually taken lightly. Hope and optimism usually foreshadow this courageous act, because a person might have to leave behind more than just material things; migrating from one's home often means leaving behind the old familiar faces -- friends and family members.

For those who lived under dictatorships, when expressing one's opinions can mean having to literally lose one's tongue or face death the thought of living in a free foreign land such as Canada can seem inviting indeed. Whatever problems may lie ahead diminish in one's mind. For others, migration might be motivated less by the push of economic or political necessity than by the pull of opportunity. This is often the case with immigrants who come to Canada as investors or arrive with the view to educating themselves in order to increase their options in life. The place from which the immigrant might have come may not necessarily be the picture of comfort but tearing oneself away from one's closest associates, whether by choice or necessity, is hardly ever an easy thing to do. For some, migration, or more appropriately, flight is the only real solution to the problems they face; thus, without projecting a positive image upon the intended destination how could one make such a difficult move?

Before coming into the country you may have seen pictures of Canada; the country is really that beautiful. As you travel around you are certain to be impressed, and watching ordinary Canadians going about their business, truck drivers and students, office workers and loiterers, you already have a sense that you are in good company with such a polite, sometimes laidback but hardworking people. The warmth and generosity of Canadians will touch your heart and you'll pat yourself on the back for having made such a brilliant decision to come to the second largest country in the world, after Russia.

As Adrienne Clarkson, former Governor General of Canada, writes in the article "An immigrant's progress," "Being an immigrant has many advantages besides optimism. For one thing, if you immigrate to Canada, you find that you have more space than you know what to do with. This was an enormous advantage to our family, and we quickly seized upon it after settling in Ottawa, building a cottage nearby in Quebec as soon as we had any savings and spending summers fishing, boating and living in the wilderness."

The Best Country in the World

So says the United Nations, over and over again, year after year. Canadians themselves may not always fully appreciate what a treasure they have in their country, but a comparative analysis of countries across the world has consistently resulted in the United Nations' rating of Canada as the number one country in the world. Even when Canada has slipped from the top spot it has remained near the top, ensuring that people who are in the pangs of economic or political distress around the world continue to see the Great White North as the place where their hopes for peace and prosperity are sure to be realized. Canada has become, to many people, a land that is synonymous with hope. From Afghanistan through Tunisia to Zambia, Canada also symbolizes freedom and the fulfillment of cherished dreams. Each year, in countries around the world, people plan, scheme, and do whatever it takes to land in Canada. In the old days, the Chinese referred to Canada as Gold Mountain (*gam san*), a term that captured the sum of the migrants' hopes for success in this land. Such hopes for financial success in Canada continue to be a motivating force for thousands of immigrants. But material needs are not the only draw. The vast prairies, the hills and hillocks, lakes and rivers, and even the uninhabited frozen fringes of the Canadian north all give comfort to the weary masses cramped in refugee camps in Sudan and the back-broken farmer in China, that somewhere on God's green earth there is a land, and kindness enough to embrace them: Canada. While stories abound of immigrants making it big financially others have found the peace of mind that this country offers to be wealth in itself. Not waking up to the rat-tat-tat of gunfire or the piercing cries of the maimed may be enough to make one declare Canada a paradise.

Peace of Mind

Two Nigerian doctors who have worked in Africa, England, the Caribbean, and the United States have found a haven for their medical practice in Canada. In the United States they had to be on guard all the time against the possibility of violence. The two, Dr. Onochie Aghaegbuna and Dr. Didi Emokpare met following their graduation in Nigeria and both, while practicing south of the border, faced threats of lawsuits and physical harm from patients and drug addicts alike. "Both men trained in U.S. emergency departments and Dr. Emokpare still works about 10% of the time in the Pasqua Hospital emergency room in Regina. But Dr. Aghaeghuna lost his desire for ER work partly because of an incident when an assailant burst into the Washington hospital ER to finish off an injured patient. The assailant fired four shots before security officers could shoot the attacker" (Driver 2003).

For some immigrants, coming to Canada then is not just a matter of making more money. Doctors in the United States can make more money but because of the possibility of malpractice suits and other threats a doctor might not necessarily sleep well at night nor be relaxed by day. According to Dr. Aghaegbuna some doctors in America find it very frustrating dealing with Health Management Organizations (HMO). HMOs control thousands of health centres, clinics, and hospitals across the United States and because the bottom line is all important doctors often need to seek permission from HMO management in order to perform some procedures for their clients. The HMOs maintain control by not so subtly reminding doctors who threaten to go on strike about the need to observe the Hippocratic Oath! Do No Harm!

Not surprisingly, not a few doctors in the United States who are working under

HMOs are fed up. Even though these two Nigerian doctors are earning less in Canada compared to the United States they understand that there is a price to pay for their choice. "If lower taxes are what you look at, you go to the States," said Dr. Aghaegbuna. But the trade off here is a more comfortable life. "Your quality of life is obviously better," added Dr. Emokpare. "At the end of the day, it's not really about the money. For the peace of mind I have working here, I'll take a pay cut" (Driver 2003). Reflecting on his experiences practicing in many countries around the world, Dr. Emokpare maintains that medical practice in Canada is the real deal. Even though he is used to moving around he believes that Saskatchewan is a place where he can live for a long time.

CHAPTER TWO

SUCCESSFUL RACIAL AND CULTURAL MINORITIES

Her Excellency Michaëlle Jean, 27th Governor General of Canada: Prepared for Service

If Canadians were thrilled to see Ms. Adrienne Clarkson, a Canadian of Chinese ancestry, in Rideau Hall, the Governor General's residence in Ottawa, the appointment of her successor, Her Excellency Michaëlle Jean, should dispel any doubts about where immigrants in Canada belong – as much in the centre as every other Canadian, although from the margins unlike other Canadians.

Immigrants – who have chosen Canada – need not whittle down their dreams simply because they were not born in this country or are still in the margins of Canadian society.

Originally from Haiti, which is often presented in the media as a place of despair, Ms. Jean could have allowed herself to be constrained psychologically by her origins. Rather, she has affirmed, or proven, that where you come from need not determine how far you can go.

Canadians increasingly appreciate that we, or our ancestors, may have come from somewhere else but that in this place we call home, Canada, we are all one, and that by working together we can continue to make Canada an example of oneness in a world of division and discord.

Ms. Jean's fluency in five languages, French, English, Italian, Spanish, and Creole, reveals more than her intelligence; she clearly knows the enriching value of the different cultures that make up our world. In addition, her pursuit of further education in linguistic and literary studies at the University of Perouse, the University of Florence, and the University of Milan, following her Bachelor of Arts in Italian and Hispanic languages and literature and a Master of Arts in Comparative Literature at the University of Montreal, points to a passion for knowledge and mastery. Ms. Jean, however, did not cloister herself in an ivory tower; she worked for almost a decade to improve the lot of battered women in Quebec, and later, as a journalist and broadcaster, she had a platform from which to enlighten Canada and the world about various social issues.

It is no accident that Ms. Jean was appointed Governor General of Canada. Here's a woman who did not allow her academic excellence to constitute a barrier between herself and ordinary Canadians such as the women whose broken lives she helped mend. And she did not fearfully sit at the margins of the society, uncertain of her place in it. Rather, through her service Ms. Jean recognized that as a Canadian she is called to join with her fellow citizens, from all backgrounds and stripes, to move Canada ever forward towards the ideal of unity, a Canada that is truly one; a Canada that shines in all its colourful array.

Adrienne Clarkson, 26th Governor General of Canada

Perhaps there is no better evidence of the opportunities that await immigrants in Canada than that of Adrienne Clarkson, who arrived in Canada as a child refugee from Hong Kong; this was during World War II when Hong Kong was occupied by Japanese soldiers. Clarkson assumed the role of Governor General of Canada in 1999, and as a representative of Queen Elizabeth II, Canada's monarch, Clarkson was essentially the nation's head of state. In her position, she was consulted by the Prime Minister and members of cabinet; of course, on the surface it may not have appeared as though she had any real power, but as Mark Bourrie reports in the article "Former Refugee Crashes Old Boys Club," (Interpress Service March 1, 2000), the Governor General has the power to dismiss the government if in her judgment, it no longer enjoys the confidence of Parliament. It is not surprising that Adrienne Clarkson's elevation to the position of Governor General has delighted immigrant and women's groups. Margaret Lo, chair of the Canada-Asia Association of Canada noted following Clarkson's appointment: "She is the first refugee to be head of state of a major Western country. That sends a great message to the world... She is also a brilliant woman, the best person for the job" (Bourrie 2000). Another Canadian, famous feminist Judy Rebick, commented that not only would Clarkson sweep out the cobwebs from Rideau Hall but also the appointment reminds people that no longer is Canada the property of the 'old boys' who controlled the country for so long (Bourrie 2000).

When Clarkson's family arrived in Canada in 1942, both as immigrants and refugees, they did not have much in the way of material goods. They had to start from scratch but rather than bemoan their lot they saw opportunity and determined to go for it. Clarkson writes in the *Maclean's* article, "An Immigrant's Progress" that next to her family's influence, she counts her experiences in the public schools and universities that she attended as having had the most critical effect on her life. She also noted that her parents felt grateful that education in Canada was affordable compared to Hong Kong where education was so costly (Clarkson 2001).

Today, immigrants from Somalia, Albania, and Mexico may be telling their children to study hard and participate fully in Canadian life so that, like Adrienne Clarkson, they too can become an inspiration to future generations of Canadians.

Clarkson did not get to where she is today by being a wallflower or a couch potato. As a former broadcaster she has a record of success behind her and though she has sometimes been considered controversial, in a free society such as Canada, it is hardly a sin to be fully engaged in the kind of debates that help to shape and reshape the thinking of society. Speaking up means moving Canadian society forward towards a progressively better social environment. Clarkson understood, even as a child, that "It was expected that the immigrant, along with everyone else, would join in the social process, which was democratic and directed towards others" (Clarkson 2001). Being a shrinking violet in Canada would not help you get what you want. Any good ideas for making Canada a better place? Make your voice heard.

Alfred Bader

Alfred Bader is a very successful businessman and a generous philanthropist. Bader was one of several hundred Jewish refugees who had arrived from Vienna, Austria over 60 years ago. Though he had come to Canada as a penniless 16-year-old, he eventually graduated from Queen's University in Kingston, Ontario, going on to earn a doctorate from Harvard before starting a Milwaukee-based business that became one of the leading suppliers of research chemicals. As Sonja Sinclair reported in the May 15, 2000 issue of *Maclean's* magazine under the title, "No Ordinary Campers," Bader later started an international art dealership, which now deals in about 200 paintings annually, "including multimillion-dollar masterpieces by Rembrandt and Rubens. In addition to Bader's generous donation to Victoria College, his wife's alma mater, he has given, over the years, some $30 million to Queen's." In 1999 he donated a couple of million dollars to the University of Toronto.

Bader's success is just one of many from immigrants who "accidentally" ended up in Canada. The refugee group that included Bader had actually not sought to come to Canada. In the end, however, they turned out to be a great gift to the nation. During World War II the British government apprehended them believing they were Nazi sympathizers. Bader and the others were not even aware of where they were being taken until they sailed up the St. Lawrence River in July of 1940. The immigration director at the time, F.C. Blair, warned about the release of those refugees in Canada; while they were allowed into Canada they were promptly locked up for between two and three years. Prior to their release, they were given the choice of either going to school or assisting the war effort. Of these immigrants that Blair warned about, over seventy ended up as university professors, two of whom won the Nobel Prize. Many of the almost one thousand people from this group of refugees who decided to make Canada their home have enriched the cultural fabric of the nation through vocations and avocations such as writers, researchers, and musicians (Sinclair 2000).

The immigrants who are coming to Canada today, like Bader and his group, may have their own aspirations and contributions to make to Canadian society. Bader and his cohort would not have been able to achieve what they did if they had been prevented from taking advantage of educational opportunities in the country.

Ujjal Dosanjh, Federal Minister of Health

Mr. Dosanjh was born in India and lived in England when he was a teenager. He immigrated to Canada in the late 1960s. Like many Canadian students today, Ujjal worked full-time while attending university. He received a Bachelor's degree in political science from Simon Fraser University and later a law degree from the University of British Columbia. Mr. Dosanjh was called to the British Columbia Bar in 1977 and practiced law successfully until the early 1990s when he entered provincial politics. After a few years' experience as a Member of the Legislative Assembly of British Columbia, he became the province's minority Attorney General. Mr. Dosanjh made history in 2000 when he became the first visible minority premier of British Columbia, the first in Canadian political history. Perhaps, more from the mismanagement of his party in years past than from his own failings, Dosanjh and his government were subsequently defeated by the Liberal Party, headed by former Vancouver mayor, Gordon Campbell. Mr. Dosanjh returned to rebuilding his law practice but was soon called by Canadian Prime Minister Paul Martin to stand as a candidate for the Federal Liberal Party. In 2004, Dosanjh was rewarded with a cabinet level post, as the Minister of Health for Canada. Dosanjh's life, to date, gives evidence of the opportunities that await immigrants who work hard, focus on clear goals, and have access to strategic resources such as education, appropriate network and community support.

Other Canadian Immigrant Success Stories

Yousuf and Malak Karsh

Yousuf and Malak Karsh embody the highest levels of photographic excellence. Refugees from the brutal 1915 Turkish genocide against ethnic Armenians, the two brothers chose Canada. Their uncle, who owned a portrait studio in Sherbrooke, Quebec, encouraged them to follow in his footsteps. In addition to photographing Winston Churchill, thanks to a sitting made possible by Prime Minister Mackenzie King, Yousuf photographed such highly-acclaimed individuals as Franklin D. Roosevelt, Ernest Hemingway, Charles de Gaulle, John F. Kennedy, and Nikita Khrushchev (Yousuf Karsh 2001). Malak, who had worked as an assistant to his brother, eventually, also made a name for himself as an outdoors photographer (Yousuf Karsh 2001). The dedication, talent, and professionalism of the Karsh brothers brought them personal glory but the accolades extend to Canada where these two men achieved their success. If Canada had not provided such a fertile soil for their ambitions, the Karshes may not have been able to bloom and blossom and share with the world their gifts and talents as photographers.

Mano Sandhu

Mano came to Canada from India in 1975 with two Master's Degrees and $8 in her pocket. She graduated from High School in India when she was 13, received her Bachelor's degree at 17 and her first Master's degree at 19. Having no job she began to get involved in her small community in Salt Spring Island, British Columbia, by offering to teach Indian cooking lessons. After a short time she decided to commute to the University of Victoria to take a Master's in Public Administration. She did this while working part time in an old people's home and raising two young children. It was hectic but she kept her goal in mind and was very determined to achieve it. Since she earned the degree in 1988 she has been working steadily. She did some consulting work with BC Systems Corporation, started her own import/export business, and has been working for the British Columbia provincial government. Apart from Mano's hard work, individual intelligence and personal ambition, her success is also connected to the chance a manager in one of the Government Ministries in British Columbia gave her to start her public service career.

Tak Wah Mak

At the age of 15, Tak Wah Mak left China to study in the United States. He later moved to the University of Alberta in Edmonton to complete his doctorate in biochemistry. As a *Maclean's* article on Tak Wah Mak notes, in the early 1970s, at the Toronto-based Ontario Cancer Institute, Mak began path-breaking research that focused on the immune system. He "captured the world's attention in 1984 with his discovery of T-cell receptors--the highly specialized parts of virus-fighting cells that help keep the human body free of infection. The potential implications of Mak's research for the treatment and prevention of not only some forms of cancer, but also HIV/AIDS, are still unfolding" ("Tak Wah Mak [BrainGain]" 2001). For people like Mak who could have made a lot of money in other places such as the United States there must be something special about Canada that encourages them to make it their permanent abode.

Freedom and Success

When Ms. Emmie Leung arrived in Winnipeg in 1972 from Hong Kong she could not believe how cold the winters were in that part of Canada. Following her graduation from the University of Winnipeg with a Bachelor's degree in business administration she worked as a temporary worker in a large company. Her take-charge attitude was not welcomed. Wondering what to do she sought counsel from family members back in Hong Kong. Even though her father suggested she return to Hong Kong Ms. Leung refused. Driven by her determination to be independent she cast her eyes upon the vast Canadian business landscape for some opportunities.

Leung saw Canada as a land of opportunity – a place where she felt she could succeed free of the gender stereotyping of her homeland. It was her desire for freedom that originally led her to Canada, she says. She credits her brother with first suggesting that she start up a recycling company. "My family was in recycling," she says. "I said to myself, 'That is where my interest is. Nobody {here in Canada} had this business yet.' I confess, I did not have the vision {that recycling would be a wave of the future.} I did it by default. No employers wanted me."

(Chinese Businesswoman Finds Freedom and
Success in Vancouver's Rubbish…1994)

After doing her costing on transportation, Leung realized that it would be profitable to ship paper to Asia's Pacific Rim. In 1976, at 25 years of age, she started her business with two employees, $15,000 and a van. Initially, she purchased and shipped bales of paper that she bought in Canada. To increase the volume she convinced local politicians to let her provide homes in a few communities with blue bags that would hold old newspapers. Curb side recycling has become very much a part of everyday Canadian life but in 1982 Ms. Leung's idea was Canada's first successful attempt at municipal curb side recycling. "Today, Leung's company employs more than 100 people at five collection centres that annually process more than 100,000 tons of paper, plastic, and metal for shipment to wherever she can get the best price" (Chinese Businesswoman Finds Freedom and Success in Vancouver's Rubbish…1994). What does Ms. Leung like about Canada besides making money from recycling? "I always looked forward to Western-style living, gender equality – that is the prime factor that motivated me," she says. "The freedom. That's what I love most about Canada" (Chinese Businesswoman Finds Freedom and Success in Vancouver's Rubbish…1994).

CHAPTER THREE

GOING FOR THE GOLD

Enough About Other People's Dreams; What About Yours?

No doubt, you have your own dreams. You may be having visions of buying a home, starting a business, or in the very near future, making a million dollars! For now, however, more pressing concerns may include finding a place to stay, a base from which you can transform your dreams into reality. To be sure, you would not be the first person to have come to Canada with the belief that the intelligence, tenacity, maturity, and other personal qualities that made you a success in your country and helped you survive what might have been a treacherous journey to these parts would also help you to succeed. Unfortunately, this has not always been the case. Such overconfidence has been the undoing of many an immigrant. Far too many have been blindsided in the benign looking environment of Canada, forcing them to abandon their dreams and to accept conditions of life that they would never have imagined a few years before. Not taking the time to understand the Canadian system and the underlying rules that govern life can be pricey in the long run. Taking the time to study the lay of the land, so to speak, will save you from the kind of mistakes that have sidelined many and turned them into bitter wrecks with nothing good to say about Canada.

Regardless of the motivation for migration, the excitement of living in Canada may have meant not giving enough thought to what the realities might be. You may have heard only the stories of milk and honey and those about the big, bright, boulder of gold that glistens through the four seasons, beckoning to all. While the potential immigrant might have acquired some information about the target country, there is no guarantee that such information will always match up with the reality. It is no doubt disappointing, for example, for people who envisioned living amiably in a new environment to find that not all neighbours are welcoming and that not everyone is happy to see them around.

Your First Year

Your first year in Canada might be one filled with emotions. On the one hand, you have exciting opportunities and challenges awaiting you, while on the other hand, you might look back with nostalgia on some of the more precious elements you left behind including the positive memories you have of your home country. Even though Canada may have extended a welcoming hand to you, it is possible that as an immigrant you will find yourself "in a social environment that is confusing, frustrating, and challenging. In most cases [immigrants] will find that holding the status of "immigrant" does not enhance their identity nor does it facilitate their ability to integrate into the host society" (Frideres 2002). You might feel that the best way to get a handle on your new life is to ponder about it from the safety of your room, home, or apartment. Whereas back home you may have been a minor celebrity in your neighbourhood, here in Canada you may be invisible even if you are a so-called visible minority! In your home country your brilliance may have blinded your teachers, parents, and friends but in Canada there are times when, in your dealings with people, you might wonder if they are not perhaps questioning your intelligence. Considering that even those who come to Canada with some French or English speaking ability sometimes have communication challenges the problem may be compounded for those who do not have the benefit of speaking one or the other of Canada's two official languages: English and French. Do not hold yourself back, however, because of uncertainty about your use of one of Canada's official languages.

It may seem safe to stick close to your own community whether in terms of race, ethnicity, religion or language. This is especially the case for those who have the benefit of a large ethnic community within which they can operate. For example, a Chinese living in Vancouver may be able to interact in the main with people from his or her background. It is possible to visit a Chinese doctor, eat Chinese food, speak Chinese on an almost daily basis and thus feel that there is really no need to interact with other Canadians. Young people, at any rate, sometimes find it much easier to embrace the notion of being Canadian, sometimes even rejecting the norms of their ethnic or national background. Even after you have become a citizen you might still have to answer questions related to your origins. In this matter, some are proud to identify their backgrounds while others might wonder why there is such a great emphasis on people's origins. After all, aren't we all now committed to Canada?

Don't Prejudge

Just as you do not want people to prejudge you, give others the benefit of the doubt. Approach people with a positive expectation and you're likely to be met with open arms. Making assumptions about people is dangerous. You may have heard stories of prejudice; don't let that deter you because not everyone is prejudiced. If you need a job, go for it. Do not hold back on the assumption that you might not get it. If you approach any situation with confidence, you increase your chances manifold. A positive attitude is likely to take you much farther in Canada than a negative attitude will. Sometimes, it is possible to win simply by not entertaining the idea of failure. In any case, Canadians are far from being perfect. Thus, in some cases, one has to fight for one's rights.

Be Aware

In Canada's politically correct environment one has to continually pay attention to one's choice of words. Don't be surprised if someone snarls at you for using the word "disabled," for example, which you know to be a perfectly good English word. "Physically-challenged" is the politically correct term. To avoid being accused of sexism you might want to say fire fighter instead of fireman, police officer instead of policeman. Resist the urge, however, to say, "person-hole" for manhole. Immerse yourself in your new environment and feel free to debate with other Canadians while remaining sensitive to others' feelings.

You Can Achieve Your Dreams

Though Canada holds much promise for personal success and achievement, so often, people have come to Canada only to have their grandiose dreams shattered. It is not uncommon to see immigrants who have been in the country for, sometimes upwards of twenty years, feeling bitter at the "system" and at Canadians for erecting so many overt and covert barriers that the immigrant has virtually no chance to transform his dreams into reality. Some give up, cutting down their original vision to size and taking to existing on the back streets of society, as faceless, anonymous drones. Others may keep their hopes alive though the stark gap between their current state and their grandiose dreams may make one question the sanity of holding on to those dreams. There are also those who come with an ironclad will and determination that no matter how long it takes and how many setbacks they face they would achieve their goals. They may go through years of trial and error or if fortunate, find a legitimate shortcut to reaching the goals they have set for themselves. What are the elements that can help an immigrant, new to the land or not, navigate the Canadian social and economic waters in order to arrive safely at the port of personal and professional prosperity? Even under the best of circumstances, personal initiative is necessary. And if you are banging your head against a brick wall, could it be that you have to redirect your efforts? Do you have a strategy for success or are you just drifting along? A person who just drifts along has not much choice about where he or she ends up. You might have to take a more proactive approach or redirect your energies in order to reap the rewards you deserve.

IDA: Renew Your Commitment to Success

Having talent and confidence is not enough. Even education is not always the answer to the achievement of goals though it can make a person more aware and open up opportunities. Not everyone who has come to the country with a degree or a head full of knowledge has been able to transmute such knowledge into personal success, satisfaction, or happiness. Immigrants who have smelled the sweet fragrance of success in their native land may respond with frustration to what may seem like endless roadblocks in Canada. For some, time, the acquisition of knowledge about their environment and a good plan are what may eventually transform their dreams into reality. No matter what skills an immigrant brings to Canada, it is worth noting that the waters here may be completely different from what one might have known in one's own country. Canadian society, the Canadian waters may seem calm and benign but never forget that still waters run deep. There are such powerful maelstroms as racism and ageism, all of which can render the unprepared paralyzed. How you respond to these unexpected societal traps can be crucial. Some choose to leave while others choose to stick it out and find ways around the challenges. While we may take inspiration from past successes, we cannot rest on our laurels and let the successes of yesteryear lull us into inaction. New environments call for new initiatives. New challenges call for new reserves of determination. And rather than assuming that we know all that there is to know, sometimes, a little bit of humility, taking the Socratic pose, and learning anew what we might have assumed we knew may help us to make new distinctions and to tackle life with a little less dread and a greater chance for success. The key then to sailing smoothly through the Canadian waters is first to be **INFORMED**, the first point of the IDA principle. Next is to be able to make definite **DECISIONS**, and finally, to take **ACTION**.

Be Informed

In order to become well informed, one has to shed one's coat of pride. It is true that you may have studied about Canada in primary school and followed news about Canada long before coming into the country. Once in the country, this process should not stop. While it is important to observe, it is also necessary to talk to others. While people from a similar background to yours can give you some insights into their personal experiences, it would be a mistake to assume such a one-sided perspective. For every immigrant who rails at the system and complains about how terrible Canada is, you might find another who seems, at least on the surface, to have found the secret to his own personal success within the very same system that is cutting others off at the knees. Rather than getting stuck within one's community it may be a good idea to seek ideas from different sources. Some immigrant groups have done quite well because they share critical information with people in their circle, thus saving newcomers years of headache. In seeking information, talk to both those who have had challenges and those who have succeeded. Sometimes they'll be one and the same. It is probably better though to steer clear of those who see no light at the end of the tunnel. Talk to those who have been able to achieve their goals and find out what they may have done to put their dreams and goals on course in spite of roadblocks. Talk with Canadians from different backgrounds; some will go out of their way to help you.

Collect brochures, newsletters, and other pieces of information, and take the time to read them as they may hold key pieces of information that could fill in for you the puzzles and perplexities of being a new immigrant.

Be Decisive

Some immigrants just go with the flow. They accept whatever life throws at them. In some cases, this works quite well. A series of happy coincidences can land someone where he or she wants to be. But one cannot always count on such coincidences. Is it not better to have a solid plan, albeit one that is flexible enough that it can accommodate any interesting detours? For some, working in a factory is the way to go. If they are fortunate enough to land a job in the field of their choice then all that is left is working as hard as they can and advancing through the ranks. But how far can you go on that route? For others, self-employment is the key. In this regard, the range of possibilities is immense. While some are able to transmute business skills into success in Canada, for others, it is necessary to continue the process of learning. Such knowledge can be acquired not only from the Internet but also from books, community colleges, and various government agencies. For still others, however, the best strategy may be committing to an academic path.

Part II of this book provides some tried and tested strategies that can help you succeed in your academic career. More than that the skills presented will help you develop critical thinking skills, which can be beneficial in the world outside of academia. Make it a point to read and reread Part II with a highlighter in hand.

Now, if one makes it one's goal to be truly well informed it is possible to acquire information to no end. In life we are presented with an array of choices, some good, others bad. We continually have to decide what to do with the plethora of choices we face. And not making a decision also constitutes a decision. It is only by taking the time to reflect on one's needs that one can make the proper decisions in life. If we come to the decision to do something with our lives, we are energized to direct our activities and to take the necessary steps that would take us inexorably to that end. But we have to decide. Is going to school the best decision we can take now? Or is it better to work for a few years and save some money before taking that step? And if going to school is the goal, which type of school do we want to attend? Can we afford to go back and forth to school? Or are we better off taking a correspondence course? At some point, and the sooner the better, after gathering information, we need to decide what to do with our lives. If we have been well informed it is possible that the direction we take may differ from what we might have considered before coming to Canada. It is also possible that the information we glean from our research would confirm the wisdom of our original plan. Making our decision on a foundation of information rather than whim would make us rest easy as we go about doing what it takes to get us where we want to reach in life.

Take Action

Have you ever had the opportunity to watch a boxer in training for a bout? Okay, if boxing is not up your alley, what about a sprinter or for that matter any serious sportsperson. An athlete who is serious about winning understands the necessity for daily practice. The Japanese have a saying: *Keizoku wa chikara nari*, which translates to: Persistence is power. Action, therefore, need not be a matter for the moment only but one that is continual. Thus, an athlete might wake up every morning long before the sun is up to practice for several hours. This may be fun in itself but it may also be gruelling, raising periodic doubts as to the wisdom of embarking on what may seem like an elusive quest; and yet the determined person presses on, day after day after day, knowing that the payoff would come handsomely on the day of competition. If you have decided to go to school, do you see the goal of achieving your degree or diploma in the same light as the Olympic-bound athlete? And are you willing to press your pants to the chair and study for several hours each day as part of the preparation towards the achievement of your goal?

Or what if you are unemployed and your immediate goal is to get yourself a job. What kinds of actions are you willing to take each day towards the achievement of your goal? If you feel discouraged at the kind of responses you are getting, do not forget that an athlete in training for a competition may not come out of every training session feeling as good as gold. And yet she presses on. Burn the idea of the need to take continual action into your mind; let it rest on a foundation of informed decision making and the struggle towards personal achievement is already half won.

Operate From a Position of Knowledge

Lack of knowledge creates hesitancy. An army that does not know the capabilities of its opponents might overestimate the enemy's strength and hold back from making the critical attack. Canada is one of those countries where one can easily be overwhelmed by the sheer volume of information available. Almost every piece of information you want has been filed somewhere ready for you to access. Your starting point may be the phone. Practice **GOTT**: Get On The Telephone. A few carefully placed phone calls are likely to get you whatever information you need. And of course, the Internet is another useful source of information. In some cases, however, it is not enough to practice GOTT. You also have to practice **GOYA**: Get Off Your Ass (Kennedy 2000). This applies whether you are looking for a job, applying for entry to university, seeking scholarship funds, or thinking of starting a business. The personal contacts you build in the community can all contribute towards the achievement of your goals. It is an illusion that what you know will always get you where you want to go. Unfortunately, sometimes whom you know is just as important as what you know. So get with it – build your contacts. But as you learn from others remember that sometimes in order to get you have to give. So do not be stingy with sharing with others knowledge that you might have accumulated, whether in a particular subject area, experience from traveling or even elements of your culture. There is no better way to build bridges and connections with people than to share with them aspects of your culture – in particular with those who show genuine interest.

Take the High Road

Perhaps out of frustration or under the influence of misguided "friends," some immigrants find themselves on the wrong side of the law. This does nothing to further the goals for which you might have come to Canada. It is difficult to put your plans into motion when you are behind bars. And make no mistake, no matter how benign you might think you are, there are times when you might be provoked into doing something stupid. For example, how do you react when someone calls you by an ethnic slur? How do you react when people run away from you though in your mind there is no reason for them to? How do you react when people refuse to rent you an apartment or a house? If you have some creative ways of challenging people to come to their senses without resorting to violence all power to you. As a new entrant you might profit from finding out from those who have been around a little longer, what the best course of action is in situations that seem unusual or puzzling to you. You do not want to contribute to whatever negative images people in the mainstream might have of people from your particular background. Do you hear the word restraint? A word to the wise, as the saying goes, is enough.

CHAPTER FOUR

BARRIERS TO MINORITY SUCCESS: ETHNOCENTRISM

In the eyes of the world, Canada is an open, tolerant country that does a remarkably good job of accommodating newcomers. In our own eyes – and those of recent immigrants – we are a nation coasting on an outdated reputation.
[Carol Goar, We Cannot Let Immigrants Fail. *Toronto Star*, April 14, 2004]

Language

One of the most common barriers to success in Canada for immigrants is language. Having knowledge of English or French and being able to communicate in these two languages can give one a leg up. After all, whether in the workplace or in social encounters being able to communicate in the same language can tear down barriers. Immigrants who speak these two languages are sometimes surprised, however, that despite what they considered to be facility in the language some Canadians beg to differ. "You have an accent!" one hears over and over again, even when this accent does not particularly impede communication. Some exasperated immigrants have enrolled in accent reduction courses or made use of language tapes to "improve" their accents. Others believe that if Canadians can't accept a multiplicity of accents then too bad! Everyone, after all, has an accent. Just transport the Canadian born and bred individual to Ireland, Australia, or New Zealand and others would be saying the same of them. So, why can't Canadians simply accept the reality that everyone has an accent and that as long as people can express themselves clearly and well it should be possible to work with them?

As with most issues the individual has to make the determination as to what is the proper course. There are numerous instances, however, of immigrants who imagined that simply by living in Canada they would achieve fluency in English or French. As the years go by, however, they find that they are no closer to mastering either language than when they first came. Their exasperation continues to increase the longer they live in Canada and hear negative comments about their accent or their lack of fluency. With this in mind, some have found it necessary to enroll in language classes believing that such classes will enhance rather than detract from their goal of blending in with the Canadian mainstream. But not everyone wants to blend in if that means obliterating elements that lend uniqueness to their personalities. Canada, after all, encourages all Canadians to respect their own culture and those of others. The immigrant needs to be aware of the incredible importance of language and effective communication, however. When one of the writers was working in a provincial government ministry it was a matter of considerable wonder to him that people at the higher echelons seemed to be the better communicators. The directors, all masterful communicators, did not always have the highest credentials. Some only had a bachelor's degree while their subordinates held doctorates and master's degrees. It drove home the importance attached to effective communication in the work place even among native speakers. Speaking fluently in English and/or French with or without accent would facilitate your successful entry into the Canadian labour market. If you have the chance to improve your English or French speaking skills why not go for it? Bad English is nobody's culture and neither is atrocious French.

Qualified? Under or Over?

You are eager to work. You have the qualifications. You think that employers would be eager to hire you, especially since you see the same advertisement in the paper day in and day out -- the perfect job for you. Well, don't hold your breath. You may get the job but then again you might not. The number of real or imagined factors that can keep you from getting the job you need and deserve are legion. They may range from your lack of "good" language skills through your lack of a Canadian degree to your being overqualified! Your misfortune, indeed, may be your "choice" of birthplace, parents, the environment in which you grew up, or having too many degrees! Just such a problem faces many new immigrants. Despite their numerous qualifications such as higher educational credentials and impressive work experiences outside Canada, and sending out numerous résumés to Canadian organizations, they don't get any offers. Many Canadian organizations see such people as not having the relevant Canadian experience to be hired in high level jobs and at the same time overqualified for medium to lower level jobs. Those immigrants in this situation who get connected to the right community, network of settled immigrants or career counselling organization are made to realize that they need to get Canadian educational credentials or whittle their résumés down by not listing all their career achievements and their higher non-Canadian educational qualifications. Guess what? Such new immigrants get jobs.

Sorry, Wrong Accent

A white, Jewish and Jamaican couple, Joan and Richard Davidson, who moved to Toronto over twenty years ago found that looking just like the majority of Canadians provided no protection from experiencing the cold hands of prejudice. By the time they landed in Toronto with their three children Richard already had seventeen years of experience in the insurance industry. As Richard answered advertisement after advertisement without any luck on the job front it became obvious that something was not quite right. As Joan notes, "We knew it was because of his accent, because we realized that the reputation of the Jamaicans up here was not that great... To put it in absolute terms, they figured that he was black and they didn't want to employ him. It didn't take a genius to figure it out" (Ashante 1999). A number of years later, through some connections Richard was able to obtain an interview with an individual from a family-owned firm in Toronto. As he reports, "I had a great interview with the son, who was very satisfied with me, but when I met with the father he said, 'I'd really like to employ you because you certainly know your business, but the type of clientele that I have, they wouldn't be very happy with the phone being answered by a West Indian voice,' recalls Richard" (Ashante 1999). Interestingly, on those occasions when Richard's accent was mistaken for a South African, Welsh or Australian one, he noticed that he was much better received.

Despite the blatant prejudice against some population groups it is well worth knowing that there are many individuals who have succeeded in Canada nonetheless. For example, Raymond Chang, a Jamaican/Canadian is the multimillionaire chairman and capital partner of CI funds, which is one of the largest mutual funds in Canada. For every Raymond Chang, however, there are thousands of immigrants whose dreams may have been derailed not because they were not hardworking, educated, or enterprising but because their colour, like the mark of Cain, made them into untouchables, and thus destined to remain at the bottom rungs of Canadian society.

Foreign Credentials

You may have spent a few years in university and worked hard to obtain a degree. In Canada, this degree may not necessarily count for much in the eyes of employers. After all, it was not issued in Canada. The citing of foreign credentials may be just an excuse to refuse jobs to visible minorities. In one case, a lady who had taught for over twenty years in an Asian university tried to get a job in Canada and was told that her degrees, which included a Ph.D. and two master's degrees, would be recognized only up to high school level! After much haranguing of the authorities in her local area she was finally asked to take some courses in Canadian history, paving the way for full recognition of her undergraduate degree.

There are indications that some professional organizations try to keep immigrants out just to protect the jobs of their members. Certainly, it makes sense to require new immigrants to prove their expertise but some of the hoops immigrants have to jump through are so ridiculous that there is no better explanation than that the professional groups in question are trying not to open their field to newcomers. When Jurgen Reinhardt, a physiotherapist from Germany became a landed immigrant following his marriage to a Canadian, it seemed appropriate to set himself up in Canada doing what he knows best. He was told upfront by the Canadian Alliance of Physiotherapy Regulators that he had better not waste his money on the application fee as it was unlikely that he would be accepted. Reinhardt "has German colleagues in Vancouver who have failed in that attempt. So now he works as a gardener. 'I do not want to sound ungrateful because I am a guest here,' he says, 'but this is the biggest problem I have. It makes sense to have standards but this is protectionist. It has really gotten to me'" (Janigan 2002). And you know that something is not right when you consider the case of a doctor from Haiti who entered Canada in 1977 but could not practice until 1992. Fifteen years! (Janigan 2002).

In another case an immigrant from Bahrain who had been in charge of $1.7 billion under the Bank of Bahrain's management came to Canada only to realize that his background meant nothing to potential Canadian employers. Muneeb Fazili, like many other immigrants had been attracted to Canada as a wonderful place where he could give his children a comfortable life. Even though he had a chartered accountancy degree from India he had to find work in a Canadian company before his expertise would be recognized by the Canadian professional authorities in that field. As he notes, "People just weren't interested to speak to me or to see me. I think people just saw it as an immigrant's résumé and that was it" (Vu "From Executive to Entry Level" 2003). The upshot is that many immigrants have to accept jobs far beneath their professional capabilities. If it's any comfort, to catch up to one's former professional status, Lionel Laroche, vice-president of cross-cultural and relocation services at Toronto-based CPI/Hazel & Associates points out that, "It may take 10 to 15 years, but at that point, [the immigrants'] previous managerial experience becomes very valuable to an organization. That's because they now know how to manage Canadians as well as how to manage back in their home countries" (Vu "From Executive to Entry Level" 2003). Ten to fifteen years; are you taking notes? According to Laroche, Canadians may not be eager to hire managerial talent from outside because "We learn management from our public schools, from our university professors, from our parents, from our summer jobs" (Vu "From Executive to Entry Level" 2003). This might be a convenient excuse.

Could it be that because people in mainstream Canadian society grow up hearing about how wonderful Canada is and by extension how great Canadians are, they develop a feeling of superiority to people from other parts of the world? But then again, people from Australia, South Africa, or the United Kingdom are very quickly accepted and offered opportunities because Canadians probably feel that they are on a par with people from these countries whereas they might find it difficult to accept someone from Bahrain, India, or Burkina Faso coming into a company as a manager. Canadians may feel it's all right to take orders or guidance from an Australian, a Brit, or an American, all the better if that individual is white, but to take orders from a Burkinabe. Tsk-tsk. Thus, it might be more in keeping with the expectations of some in the mainstream society that immigrants from less favoured societies serve in lowly positions. When finally someone offered Fazili a position there was no disappointment. Tim Collins of Stafflink Solutions, who offered Fazili a job as a part-time accountant admits that he has learned a lot from Fazili as indeed he has provided some mentorship to this accountant from Bahrain. Isn't this the way it should be? People learning from one another and advancing together regardless of national background? Fazili, by the way, has since been promoted to a top position in the company. If Canadians gave more immigrants a chance maybe they would discover that having an accent does not mean that a person is dumb.

Canadian Experience

Though there may be some pressure on you to get a job, if you are in a position to volunteer, do so. This would help you learn about people in your host country and to absorb some of the values in the Canadian workplace. Such volunteer experience could also come in handy when employers begin to ask about whether you have Canadian experience. Your volunteer experience could be your bridge from untried newcomer to seasoned worker in the Canadian workplace. It seems like a catch-22 when employers would not offer you a job because you do not have the all-important "Canadian experience." But how, you wonder, can you gain Canadian experience when no one is willing to take a chance on you? You can short-circuit this chicken and egg quandary by getting some volunteer experience. In most major cities in Canada there are volunteer agencies. Check in the phone book or ask your friends and neighbours about such opportunities. This may be just the bridge you need to make an entrée into Canadian work life.

Now, what is so different about accounting in Canada that a professional accountant with 22 years of experience in the United Kingdom cannot pick up on the job within a matter of months? The case of Selladurai Premakumaran and his bookkeeper wife, Nesamalar, is just one of a growing number that has convinced some immigrants, particularly those from visible minority backgrounds, that there is no hope for them in Canada as far as their acceptance as professionals is concerned. Selladurai is originally from Sri Lanka while his wife is originally from Malaysia. With their long years of living in the United Kingdom no one can say that they do not speak English and yet, they were repeatedly hit for the requirement of "Canadian experience." After a few years in Canada they had to work as janitors as well as stocking shelves in supermarkets to make a living.

Guidy Manman, an immigration lawyer with Toronto's Manman & Associates, commenting on the Premakumarans' lawsuit against the Canadian government suggests that one can start making contacts and seeking a position even before arriving in Canada. The only question is that if being physically present in Canada does not help with obtaining a job how would conducting a long distance job search be any better? The only possibility is that the Premakumarans would have found out sooner how grim the prospects would be for them. They could then have saved themselves the trouble of coming over. The lack of success on the part of many professionals in accessing the job market raises the question as to whether immigrants are too obsessed with working for someone. A person with some savings and that many years of experience could investigate the possibilities of working as a self-employed accountant in Canada. One might begin as a home-based business and with a track record of success expand into regular office space. Most people with a need for accounting services would not care as long as they are assured that the job would be done satisfactorily. Considering that payment will be contingent upon proper execution of the project in question no one has anything to lose. Too few recent immigrants may be considering such possibilities even though Canada has a rich history of immigrants succeeding as self-employed individuals or families.

Dealing with "Acculturative Stress"

Going from being a doctor in one's country and enjoying the status and perks that come with it to becoming a dishwasher in Canada may cause some people to stress out. Some are strong enough that they take such a come-down for what it is: a temporary condition. But as the months stretch into years one's self-esteem can take a beating. Certainly, you can draw strength from your accomplishments in the past and acknowledge that the shenanigans that Canadians use to avoid employing immigrants do not make you less than you are. While you cannot help but feel the effects it is also clear that your lack of acceptance from those who appear to hold your fate in their hands does not necessarily mean you are incompetent. There is a point beyond which you realize that it's not just because you are not a good fit for the companies to which you are applying but that there is something deeper going on. You begin to realize that, this great country, with all its shining buildings, well-scrubbed people, gleaming cars and blooming flora, also has another side, a dark side, if you will, and that as the saying goes, all that glitters is not gold. You may find comfort in commiserating with other immigrants whose own tales of woe may be worse than your own. You may even laugh through your tears and go for a walk along the beach or do a bit of window shopping to cheer yourself up. You've come to Canada with the full expectation of throwing yourself into Canadian life but how can that happen, when you are stymied at the starting gate? Without a job, how do you participate actively in the life of the community? You may begin to wonder if you had made a mistake to make Canada your new home. You want to convince yourself that all will be well. What a beautiful country! Why can't you also have a little share in this piece of heaven on earth? But you need to get a job and all your efforts are turning to nil. Beauty is all around you but you can't have beauty for breakfast, can you? And when your three-year-old cries for some solid food you certainly can't say, "Hey, kiddo, look through that window pane. This is a beautiful country." You may begin to feel a certain disconnection between yourself and other Canadians, that is, those that you perceive to be shutting doors of opportunity in your face.

You might draw hope from the experiences of other immigrants who have eventually succeeded in making their dreams come true. For some, having an exit strategy has been the key to saving their sanity and their pocketbook. While some, such as the astronaut husbands of Hong Kong and Taiwan are able to fly back and forth between their native land and their newly adopted country not everyone is able to do so. Consider the full range of options open to you, including whether or not to accept a temporary job while doing what is necessary to gain the necessary occupational foothold in your field.

Move from Knowledge to Wisdom

Wisdom is the application of knowledge. Thus, knowing the importance of good communication skills and the concern that some employers raise about accents would you consider doing something about your accent or do you see that as an assault on your identity to have to try speaking "like a Canadian?" If you are independently wealthy and do not need to depend on others for jobs or other favours you might decide that your accent is just fine, thank you. Others might think that for the sake of adaptability it is important to work on their accents. Some Canadians may truly be unable to understand your accent even though in your heart of hearts you believe that you are speaking English or French. While some make an extra effort to understand the immigrant others take the attitude that immigrants had better adapt, or else! If you have been imagining all along that living in Canada is going to be an easy ride you might have to do a reappraisal. The reasons employers can cite for not taking you on are numerous and they do not all necessarily hold water. The common heritage of mainstream Canadians and those from Western Europe may be one of the key reasons those individuals are given opportunities much faster but the truth may be a little more complex. The educational systems of countries such as the United Kingdom and the United States are perceived to be roughly similar to the Canadian educational system whereas in many other countries Canadians are not really sure. Of course, if business leaders have been paying attention they will know that despite what they read in the media there are many other countries with a good educational base. Also, people from Europe may have more reference points with Canadians in terms of interest in popular culture. It is easier to get along with people who watch the same types of movies, enjoy the same kinds of jokes, and have the same kinds of hobbies. In a perfect world this should not have been the case but we do not live in a perfect world. So, how about taking part in activities that put you in contact with mainstream Canadians? Some have found involvement in church activities, the art and theatre scenes, or sports to be good places to connect with others.

CHAPTER FIVE

BARRIERS TO MINORITY SUCCESS: RACISM, IDENTITY, AND DIVERSITY

Thank You, Canada

Most immigrants feel grateful that Canada has allowed them in. This reflects many immigrants' awareness that Canada is indeed a terrific country. But whether immigrants or refugees many of these new entrants are very much aware of their capacities, abilities, and potential, which they do not wish to waste languishing in Canada year after year without any opportunity to contribute meaningfully to the continued development of the country. While the political asylum granted by Canada allowed them to escape from possible premature death they were also hopeful that they would be able to access jobs or take advantage of educational opportunities or self-improvement. Many, however, find out that their qualifications count for nothing or very little in Canada. Many in this group believe that racism is at the heart of their lack of economic progress or social acceptance. This is because the educational attainments of many of these new entrants to Canada are quite high, with many having completed high school and not a few with degrees or other higher educational qualifications from their old countries. Canada, by showcasing its acceptance of refugees, is able to enjoy the accolades that come with such an expression of concern for the victims. Canada is able to make a show of being beneficent which hardly translates into practice, except for those new entrants that connect to strategic resources. Even while these visible minorities lament the lack of any visible opportunities for themselves they express the hope that in time they would not forever remain at the bottom of the Canadian social and economic totem pole.

Job Search: Of Hope and Despair

Immigrants are found working in many areas of Canadian life, both the public and private sectors. For example, it is possible to find immigrants ensconced in government jobs, federal, provincial, and municipal. Immigrants have found employment as university professors, accountants, researchers, and as managers. Despite this reality, however, many other immigrants, after venturing into the workplace and finding rejection after rejection, cannot help but wonder if some other forces are not at work behind the smiles and praises of human resources staff.

Racism with a Smiling Face

One African immigrant who has taken course after course in the hope of improving his prospects comments that whenever he presents his résumé to a recruiter, invariably, he hears the comment: "Wow, you've done a lot!" and yet the phone call that would offer him a job in his field of studies never comes. As such, he has had to make do with whatever job he can find to support his family. Some immigrants are not averse to accepting any job to keep the wolf from the door. But it is only natural that someone who has spent many years preparing for a career expects to work in that field, and yet, for many immigrants, this can be a perennially elusive goal. As such, some find themselves on a perpetual treadmill of taking course after course in the hope that the tide will turn, only to find out that the prospects remain the same -- grim. Under such circumstances it is not surprising that some of these immigrants begin to have that sharp sinking feeling that the fault is not a lack of preparation or education on their part but something else, which is to say -- racism? There is definitely a limit to the practice of diversity in the Canadian workplace. Even though jobs routinely emphasize that minorities should apply and indicate their minority status, some minorities have been wondering and whispering among themselves if this is not just a ploy to quickly weed them out from the pool. As in the United States, the so-called people of colour, are more likely to be living in poverty than their white Canadian counterparts. The income gap also speaks volumes about the disconnection between the rhetoric of equality and the reality. In the upper echelons of Canadian society, few immigrants or non-Whites can be found. Whether in the provincial legislatures or the national legislature, the story is the same, few immigrants or people of colour are represented. Canada needs to translate the talk of equity and diversity into the walk of equity and diversity.

Whose Loss?

It is unlikely that many immigrants come to Canada with visions of dining with the Queen or her representative as their foremost priority. Some immigrants come to Canada to seek better economic opportunities or to escape oppression of one kind or another at home. It is very disconcerting therefore when they find that they have exchanged oppression of one kind for a more benign but no less insidious one. While for some immigrants the issue that relegates them to the fringes may be that of colour, for others it might be their accent that blocks them from being accepted fully as workers, neighbours, or friends.

In "Invisible: Diversity in Canadian Newsrooms," Federico Barahona tells the story of Ashok Chandwani, who arrived in Vancouver from India with three university degrees and three years of experience as a journalist working with English newspapers. When he went to see the head of the Vancouver bureau of the Canadian

Press, he was offered a job -- as an elevator boy! In Toronto, the editor of the *Toronto Star* told him that as much as he would like to hire Chandwani, due to a bad experience with someone from Sri Lanka he would not take a chance. Eventually, Chandwani landed a job as managing editor of the Montreal Gazette.

Of course, for the harried immigrant who is unable to find a niche in Canadian society the pain, both emotional and financial, may be difficult to deal with. But as a society, Canadians also lose by not taking advantage of the skills of the thousands of immigrants who are enticed to come to our shores only to be left stranded. As an article in *Population Today* points out, there is substantial loss to Canada for having skilled immigrants perform menial jobs. There is a loss of about C$2.4 billion, according to Jeffrey Reitz, professor of sociology and industrial relations at the University of Toronto, for not making full use of immigrants' skills. Using 1996 census data to make a comparison between the earnings of immigrants and their Canadian-born counterparts, Reitz "found that immigrants earn on average one-half to two-thirds less for their education and experience than native-born Canadians (Cost of Underemployed Immigrants to Canada's Economy Quantified 2002).

300 Job Applications – One Offer

Though Rajesh Subramaniam's job search experience occurred south of the border, in the United States, immigrants in Canada can still learn from it. Having completed a master's in chemical engineering at Syracuse University, New York, and an MBA from the University of Texas in Austin, Subramaniam did have American experience and the necessary language skills. After applying for 300 jobs he got only one offer. Part of the reason, as Subramaniam figured out, was that as a non-U.S. citizen it would entail too much paperwork for a company to try to sponsor him. Now the head of Fedex's Canadian division, Subramaniam explains that barriers exist in the workplace because people prefer to do what is comfortable. Fedex is one of the companies that is eager to tap into the expertise of people regardless of their background. "Fedex has a high proportion of visible minorities in senior management positions – almost 75. It doesn't have a quota system, but about 19 nationalities are represented at its Mississauga, Ontario, headquarters" (Robin 2004).

After sending out 500 résumés in Canada with no success, Rezaur Rahman, an immigrant and computer engineer with training from Bangladesh and China, figured that Canadians possibly think that immigrants are only here to do the jobs that they do not want to do. Rezaur thinks that this is a very backward attitude. "This is ridiculous. Everything we import comes from the countries that train the people immigrating to Canada. It's a contradiction to say we trust the things they make and not the people who make them" (Immen 2004).

Becoming fixated on racism as the only barrier to success in Canada could prevent you from considering areas of your life over which you have control and which you can improve to increase your chances of success in society.

Systemic Discrimination

Few Canadians would admit to being racists but in their hiring practices it seems clear that minorities are not favoured. This explains why even in the federal public service the number of minorities is small. A task force set up to examine government hiring practices came up with the magic figure that 20% of all new hires in the public service should be minorities. Despite this recommendation there is no indication that government departments are competing with each other to comply. Whilst some would chalk this state of affairs to more of the racism that runs through Canada's history it seems that the matter of comfort once again enters the picture. According to Ranjit Perera, who filed a suit against the Canadian International Development Agency (CIDA) for denying him a promotion he believes he deserved, systemic discrimination continues because employers and hiring managers do not have the motivation to the bottom line that those in the private sector have. Moreover, "People are always suspicious of people they are unfamiliar with or that are different from themselves, he said. It is not that they are intentionally racist. 'In the public sector where you don't have to go on the basis of looking for the person who will help you with the bottom line, you hire a person who you are comfortable with and the person you are comfortable with is a person like you'" (Brown 2001).

In addition, the structures that exclude visible minorities from jobs and positions seem to operate on the age-old expectation that some races or groups of people are inferior to others. Thus, people from such "inferior" groups, no matter what their educational background or abilities are not deemed worthy of occupying certain "high" positions. An extension of this is the stereotyping of people and associating them with particular types of jobs. Minorities who have immigrated to Canada may have been business leaders, local chiefs, religious leaders, or politicians in their home country. It is unfair of those in the mainstream to assume that every minority is either no good or up to no good. That office cleaner you pass every day on your way home used to be a government minister in Ghana. That taxi driver who took you to the hospital the other day used to be a doctor in Gujarat, and that dental hygienist who cleaned your teeth is actually a dentist from Manila. "This is a bitter joke among some immigrants... The best place to have a heart attack in Canada is in a taxi, because the driver is often a trained physician" (Markusoff 2003).

Though Canada has one of the finest educational systems in the world it seems that many of us are living in a time warp, imagining that every visible minority we bump into on the street is one of those destitute, uneducated folks we see on television. If that is the image we are still carrying around in our heads then we certainly have a deficient education, having missed news of the educational revolution in India where some of the most technologically savvy graduates are coming out; we certainly do not know about the full-day study sessions of Chinese university students while our own university students are chatting it up in the campus pubs. Some universities in the United States and Canada have begun to offer courses that focus on white culture, which try to educate whites about the process involved in their "natural" assumption of privilege in society. We may not have visible minorities being lynched in Canada or crosses being burned on their front yards, but immigrants who have spent years preparing themselves for a profession and gained a measure of success in their fields in their home countries probably feel that they are being lynched in spirit for being denied equal opportunity. They die a thousand times within when they know that the rejection of their applications was not because of their incompetence but because of their national origin or the pigmentation of their skins. In this 21st century, in one of the most enlightened countries in the world, isn't it a shame that people have to be judged not by the content of their character but by how much melanin they carry in their skin?

Identity Crisis

Most people accept who they are. They may change their hairstyle from time to time or do a nose job or two, but by and large, they are comfortable in their own skin; they must accept what nature has bestowed upon them. The so-called visible minority in Canada who may never have experienced issues of identity in her home country, now finds that despite calls for respect of differences there are subtle and not-so subtle hints that her colour is the wrong one. Feeling rejected by the mainstream society some retreat into a circumscribed community whether one of race, ethnicity, religion, or language. Others may intensify their quest for acceptance by attempting to erase ineradicable aspects of their backgrounds or by distancing themselves from others in their boundary community. As Frideres (2002) explains, those who choose to remain physically and socially within the confines of a boundary community may find it easier, at least in the short run, in easing themselves into the mainstream. They have the support of the community, which can help them deal with any shocks in the system. For example, "Chinese immigrants with little or no English/French have little difficulty in carrying out business, social/recreational activities and other forms of social interaction within the Chinese community. However, when they venture into the larger society, their lack of the official languages and their lack of understanding of the cultural norms poses major hurdles for them" (Frideres 2002). Such individuals may see their boundary community as their major system of support and be drawn even more into this community where they do not have to worry about making major mistakes in their everyday interactions. As their comfort level with mainstream society rises, however, they may extend themselves beyond their boundary community.

Others may distance themselves from the boundary community in an effort to accelerate the process of integration. For some, especially the young, this may be an attempt to escape what they may perceive to be a stigma attached to their ethnicity, accent, traditional clothing styles, or religious symbols. After being partially integrated into Canadian society some individuals become confused as to where they truly belong. One fourth-generation Canadian of South East Asian ancestry, even in her late twenties, had no real conception of her identity and spoke of herself as being white. According to her, because she had gone to school with whites, had a string of white boyfriends, lived all her life in Canada she was white! It was only after a professor in her university advised her to delve into the history of South Asian immigration to Canada that she came to see the connections between herself and her ancestors who had landed on the coast of British Columbia several decades ago.

For some young people, the confusion in identity manifests itself in disagreements with their parents, who may still be very much connected to the traditions and norms of their homeland. Families have to be aware of these issues and seek positive ways of dealing with them, otherwise there is the prospect of families breaking up because of misunderstandings and the confusion that can arise from the intermingling of cultures.

Frideres (2002) notes that young immigrants, that is, those between the ages of 1 and 9, having little or no self-concept or identity, quickly become Canadians because of their flexibility and the malleability of their identity. "The extent to which this happens is a function of how linked the parents are to the collectivity to which they identify and the degree to which they expect their children to mirror the boundary community's culture. On the other hand, if the young immigrant is a "visible minority" her/his participation in Canadian society may be circumscribed by the level of prejudice and discrimination exhibited by the host society. Depending upon the social environment the young child finds her/himself within the resultant identity of the child will be quite different" (Frideres 2002).

Those between 10 and 20, who have already developed a core self-identity and basic linguistic skills may have an arrested development and "tend to become marginalized people in their new host society. They are bilingual/bicultural at best but in most cases are neither. Strong forces from multiple sources impinge upon their loyalties and thereby they create the marginal person" (Frideres 2002). Adults, with a well-developed self-identity, may understand that while they may never truly become Canadian in the sense of adopting the full range of Canadian norms, at least, they need to embrace some basic elements of the Canadian culture.

Once immigrants realize that Canadians look down upon their place of origin they may be reluctant to share this information and hope, and perhaps insist, on simply identifying themselves as Canadians. But whites find it far easier to claim to be Canadians without the pressing questions of their "true" origins unless they have a very thick accent. The so-called visible minorities have to be prepared at all times to explain where they came from. This even extends to visible minorities whose ancestors may have been pioneer immigrants, dating to a century or so back. Some blacks in Nova Scotia can trace their ancestry to the 18th and 19th centuries when through the so-called *Underground Railway* slaves came from the United States to settle in a free Canada. But some of these black Canadians, like immigrants, who came only yesterday, have to justify their being Canadian all the time. Questions about origins are not only confined to the social sphere, where one might easily sidestep it. For example, if one needs to use some government services one might be required to note place of origin. This should ordinarily not be a problem except that after experiencing so many overt and covert acts of racism one is never quite sure how such identification might be used against the individual. In the social sphere, however, one is free to take on whatever identity one sees fit. As Frideres explains, "For example, people of mixed ethnic ancestry, people of united origin can be defined in a number of ways; e.g. immigrants from Jamaica can define themselves as Canadian, Jamaican, West Indian, or black" (Frideres 2002).

Drawing the Ire of Mainstream Canadians

Since 1971, when the government of Canada set up a policy of multiculturalism, which acknowledges the right of every ethnic group to "preserve and develop its own culture within the Canadian context" some in the mainstream see the Canadian government as having lost its head. For decades the English and French descendants of the earliest settlers, along with continued immigration from Europe helped lay the foundation for the character of the nation. Granted, the character of the nation included heavy doses of racism towards Aboriginal Canadians and visible minorities, notably blacks and Asians. While many Canadians have masked their displeasure of the increasing number of immigrants and refugees with false smiles and polite indifference some of the new arrivals are raising the ire of mainstream Canadians who fear that these immigrants want Canada to change to fit them rather than the other way round. Tom McConaghy, in the article "Multicultural Policy Under Attack," cites Raheel Raza, a freelance writer and a new Canadian who reminds other immigrants in a piece written in the Globe and Mail of July 21, 1993, not to make it their priority to transform Canada. As Raza points out, "Many of us [immigrants] did not have the luxury of free medical care, workers' compensation, freedom of speech and human rights, plus all the other wonderful systems we are exposed to in Canada" (McConaghy 1995). Raza challenges immigrants to stop pushing the system to suit themselves and chides them for making mountains out of molehills.

Also, government efforts to encourage the hiring of women and visible minorities may be having a backlash as people in the mainstream, particularly white males, increasingly see themselves as losing the place of privilege that they had enjoyed since the founding of Canada. As McConaghy notes, "The number of Canadians who are disturbed by the demands being made by ethnic groups is increasing. A recent poll conducted by the federal government found that four in ten Canadians believe that there are too many members of visible minorities in Canada; they singled out Arabs, Blacks, and Asians. What was amazing about the poll was that Toronto, probably North America's most multicultural city (38% of the population from minority ethnic groups) turned out to be the intolerance capital of Canada, with 67% of respondents saying that there were too many immigrants" (McConaghy 1995). It seems that a majority of Canadians would prefer that immigrants adapt to a Canadian value system rather than hang on to their own. Demands by some immigrants that parts of the Canadian anthem be changed, that official recognition be given to their holy days, and that certain performances such as Showboat and Miss Saigon be cancelled to accommodate their sensibilities have added to the feeling that Canada is headed for trouble. Some simply say that this is evidence that the government's much-vaunted multiculturalism policy has failed.

In Richmond, B.C. where about a third of the population is of Asian extraction there are probably more rumblings from the mainstream than other communities across Canada. Fueled by money from Hong Kong, Richmond has a heavy concentration of retail shops, plazas, and malls that boast all manner of Chinese products. Some non-Asians have called it the "Asian invasion" not so much for the shopping centres with distinctly Chinese character but for the impression that members of the Chinese Community prefer to live an insular life within Canada.

Racial Profiling

Whether it is true or not that some police units around the world use images of black people for target practice many Blacks in Canada feel that they are inordinately targeted by the police. For blacks in Canada, who are said to be at the bottom of the totem pole, being stopped by the police, sometimes for apparently no reason, has become a matter of common expectation. Not a few blacks can recount an experience of being stopped by the police for the ostensible reason that they looked like someone on a criminal watch list. Some unlucky ones, according to anecdotal reports, have even been bundled into police cars in broad daylight. As Sujit Choudry explains in "Laws Needed to Ban Racial Profiling," "Racial and ethnic profiling is the use of race or ethnicity either as the sole factor, or as one factor among many, in a decision to detain or arrest an individual, or to subject an individual to heightened security. Profiling employs race and ethnicity as a proxy for the risk of committing criminal acts" (Choudry 2002). It seems that being black is sometimes enough of a trigger for some in the police to pounce. Blacks who are unable to control their anger on such occasions risk giving the police officers reason to use force against them.   In   a finding by the *Toronto Star* newspaper there was a much higher likelihood for African Canadians to be charged with traffic-related offenses compared to their mainstream counterparts. So whether in the airports, at the borders or on the streets, minorities have to be aware that because of the sins of the few among them or because of just plain racism they could find themselves targeted by law enforcement officials. Some victims have been able to press their case in court and won; others have simply accepted it as an unfortunate part of living in Canada and that walking or driving while black is one of the hazards of living in the best country in the world.

Kary Taylor, a black man living in Vancouver, British Columbia, was out on a date one evening. He was driving a nice car, with an Asian lady in the front seat. He had failed to park properly and when a police officer tried to get his attention he drove off. The police car followed him and got him to stop. When Taylor got out, the police officer pressed the barrel of the gun against his temple, leaving an abrasion. Another officer came on the scene to provide back up for the RCMP officer who was dealing with Taylor. As the backup officer, Michelle Lakusta, later testified in the court hearing against the quick-on-the-draw RCMP officer, "He said he saw a black man in a nice car with an Oriental female and, given the area, he wasn't sure if it was possibly a prostitute-pimp situation" (Bohn 2001). Kary Taylor was a dentist and could afford to buy a nice car but his colour marked him as a pimp and if he had made the mistake of resisting who knows what might have happened to him.

Racism and Violence

On a few occasions the dislike of immigrants has led to, shall we say, not-so-pleasant encounters. If the individuals who beat up Suman Chowdhury, an Indian engineer based in Quebec, had taken the time to examine his résumé they would have realized that he was quite an accomplished individual. If they had engaged him in friendly banter they would have learned that he and his family had called Quebec home for almost twenty years. But on that fateful day when Suman was humiliated in full view of other Canadians none of that mattered. For the two young women and three young men who pounced on Suman and his wife Sumita it did not matter that in his job, Suman Chowdhury had "designed the natural gas delivery system into Sherbrooke, Trois-Rivières, Chicoutimi and other cities" (Abley 2002). His colour marked him as an undesirable. "Pakis," said one of the women, "go back where you come from." She used other abusive names, too, which Chowdhury elects not to repeat" (Abley 2002). It may not happen often but for some in the mainstream the hatred of foreigners goes that deep. Suman Chowdhury was shocked that while he was being pummelled and punched and shoved no one made any attempt to intervene or plead on his behalf. If no one came to his rescue that day he was shocked still more that no public officials condemned these acts once they became public.

Longing for the Good Old Days?

Recent immigrants wonder about all the brick walls that they have to face. A kinder and gentler Canada would have jobs ready for them, furnished apartments at the ready. Considering that among the refugees and immigrants who came to the country forty, fifty, or sixty years ago, many have not only become pillars of Canadian society but have the financial clout to go with it, you may be wondering if you had come to Canada in the wrong decade. If recent immigrants have taken any time to learn about Canada's history they might well realize that they are living in the best of times! Recent immigrants can learn a thing or two from Art Patterson whose father came to Canada from England in 1889 and worked as a farmhand in a part of Canada that was part of the Northwest Territories. "My dad was one tough guy. He used to drive his produce to Calgary once each week – rain or shine, winter or summer. He rode his democrat [a horse-drawn buggy] in the summer or his sleigh in the winter. It took 2½ hours each way" (Peterson *et al* 2000). Longing for the good old days? As Patterson says, "Kids these days have the buses, and it's a darn good thing too. The only thing good about the good old days is that they are gone" (Peterson *et al* 2000). Which is why, you are probably reclining in your sofa, in a room with central heating, a television set, and your Toyota in the garage.

Having doubts about the wisdom of remaining in Canada? You may learn a thing or two from Peter C. Newman, who has been a fixture on the Canadian writing and journalism scene for decades. When World War II began Canada refused to allow Jews who were escaping from Hitler's holocaust to take refuge in the country. Businessman Oscar Neumann managed to bring his wife, Wanda, and their eleven-year-old son, Peter, to Canada thanks to a special program sponsored by Canadian Pacific Railway that allowed refugees with the necessary funds to purchase farmland belonging to the company and farm it for 5 years.

The Neumann family settled on their 15-acre plot in Freeman, Ontario, and the family, more used to living in a palatial home in Czechoslovakia, had to settle for the ramshackle structure on the farm. Meanwhile, Mr. And Mrs. Neumann worked upwards of 15 hours each day. The Neumann family could not speak English and knew little about life in Canada. They could not escape the anti-Semitism that was brewing at the time. For fear of being targeted the Neumanns put the label Dependable Fruit Growers on their farm truck which they drove to the Hamilton market every morning. According to Peter Newman, his family was made to feel less than welcome in the community in which they lived. For example, no family ever invited them and other than the Hamilton Rotary Club no other club or professional association would allow them to join. The family was devastated to hear one day that Newman's grandparents, on both sides, and many other family members had been victims of the Nazi pogroms and had been gassed. "I remember that I was plowing a celery field in the spring of 1945 when the news came in a letter from the Red Cross, and it hit me: Canada had, literally, saved my life. My passionate dream at the time was to become a Canadian, worthy of my adopted land. Now, more than a half century later, that dream is no less compelling. To be a Canadian remains my highest ambition" (Peterson *et al* 2000).

Following the bombing of Pearl Harbor by the Japanese on December 7, 1941, Japanese Canadians were branded as "enemy aliens." Over 20,000 of them, most actually born in Canada were sent to work camps and ghost towns across the country. Harry Yonekura, who was a 19-year-old fisherman at the time, was taken away from his home in Steveston, B.C., to spend a year in a prisoner of war camp in Angler, Ontario. In 1938, when his father suffered a stroke, Yonekura became the man of the house. He worked hard and by 1941 could make as much as $3,700 in a single week. To put this amount in perspective, it was enough to buy two or three luxury Buicks. Following the events of Pearl Harbor, the family's fishing boats were seized by the Canadian government. "A fisherman without a boat is no fisherman, but my country was at war, and as a Canadian I would do my best to cooperate with my government in whatever way I could" (Peterson *et al* 2000).

That was before the government started rounding up Japanese men. Canada's internment of Japanese is said to have been less humane than America's, as south of the border families were kept together. Yonekura and three others were grabbed on the street in broad daylight by RCMP officers and taken away to a camp four days' drive away. Yonekura, a Canadian citizen, could not believe that such a thing could happen to him in his own country. The RCMP would not even allow him to phone his mother to let her know what was happening to him. Yonekura managed to get his family together by 1946. Though the city was barred to Japanese Canadians the camp commander did not think too badly of him and told the district security commissioner to look after him. "The war was over but we were still kept from some cities and even needed a government license to buy homes. April 1 of 1949 is what we *Nisei* call our Freedom Day because it wasn't until then that the government lifted all restrictions on the right to vote for Japanese-Canadians" (Peterson *et al* 2000).

Strength Through Diversity

While some Canadians lament the increasing influx of immigrants from non-traditional sources others see in this development an opportunity to gain much needed competitive advantage in their business operations. One such individual who sees value in diversity is Bernard F. Isautier, CEO of Canadian Occidental Petroleum Ltd. Isautier tells the story of his first visit to Vietnam on a trade mission in which the Prime Minister took part. "In the Canadian delegation about a quarter of the business people were of Vietnamese origin. These individuals can best explain to Vietnamese authorities what Canada can do for Vietnam and what business linkages should be established" (Benimadhu 1995). Tapping into the knowledge that members of ethnic communities possess Canadian companies can more easily penetrate international markets. Isautier, who is an immigrant from France, does not see any real racism in Canada. As he notes, "If you walk down the corridors of many oil companies here in

Calgary for instance, you will see people of all origins working together without any problem, respecting one another's faith and beliefs" (Benimadhu 1995).

CHAPTER SIX

LET'S TALK ABOUT S - SOLUTIONS

Astronaut Husbands, Satellite Wives, and Parachute Children

The difficulties immigrants face in getting their credentials recognized may have contributed to the situation where some members of an immigrant family maintain a work connection with their home country. In such situations, the husband, usually referred to as the "astronaut," leaves the family behind in Canada and returns to the home country to work. Initially, the whole family might have looked forward to re-establishing themselves in Canada. But soon the reality hits that no matter what positions these individuals might have held in their native countries they are not likely to get similar positions in Canada. Naturally, to maintain the lifestyle to which they have become accustomed, it only makes sense for one or both parents to return and work, leaving the children in Canada to benefit from the opportunity of improving their English skills. Astronauts are not only found among the Hong Kong Chinese and Taiwanese. Highly educated immigrants and entrepreneurs from India, Pakistan, the United Arab Emirates, and Qatar leave their wives and children in Canada and jet back to their home countries where their skills are recognized, and along with it, the income and respect that they deserve as professionals. As Haroon Siddiqui writes, "We are following a 19th century model not the 21st – abandoning poor newcomers into pockets of poverty, while not being very attractive for the bright and well-to-do" (Siddiqui 2000).

As one so-called satellite wife explains: "If we do want to find a job here, I think most people can, but probably just a very low-end job. Probably they'll just get seven or eight dollars an hour, but in comparison to the salary in Taiwan it's... very low... Probably... we can survive here. But it won't be enough for us. People in Taiwan have a lot of savings. We feel comfortable to have a lot of savings, but we don't here... We just feel comfortable if one of the spouses can have a better job, so we can make more choices" (Waters 2003). Some mainstream Canadians claim that some of these immigrants had no intention of settling in Canada in the first place. For some immigrants, the strength to cope with perceived barriers in Canada comes from having the opportunity to interact with people who have been in the system longer and lived to tell the tale, so to speak.

The Merely Earthbound

For those who do not have the benefit of an astronaut's huge salary, sticking together as a family and planning may be the key to finding success in Canada. It is not uncommon to find some immigrant families sharing modest living quarters and saving their pennies in anticipation of the day when they might be able to buy a home of their own or set up a business; they are bound by a common purpose and an understanding of the need to sacrifice in order to achieve their goals. In some cases, however, such living conditions only aggravate the relationship especially when some in the family adapt to Canadian society faster than others. Some immigrant parents cannot understand why their children adopt the dressing styles or social posture of mainstream Canadians. At the same time some of these young people cannot understand why their parents are so restrictive in a land that promises unbounded freedom for every individual.

Be a Creative Problem Solver

As an immigrant and a minority, you might be seen by Canadians not just for who you are as an individual but as a member of a group. Now, if this group is perceived negatively, then it means you automatically inherit some of this negativity. When you go to the bank and you are asked to produce five identity cards, when you can never make any headway in your job search, you do not always have to blame yourself. It may be that you are being unfairly judged. But the question is, "What are you going to do about it?" Are you going to fight for your rights? Are you going to reappraise yourself and fill in any gaps that may exist in your background or qualifications? Do you resign yourself to the status quo or do you seek creative ways out of your predicament? Attitude, as the saying goes, can determine your altitude.

Immigrants Helping Immigrants

Most people who come to Canada, either as immigrants, international students or refugees are able to connect with some people from their background. Even though the individuals might not be family members they can still be crucial in helping one make sense of what may seem to be the confusing first few months. Eighty-seven percent of immigrants apparently have some form of social support system in Canada. "Over half (54%) of newcomers already had relatives and friends living in the country; another third (33%) had only friends. Most newcomers (78%) settled in areas where their network of friends and relatives lived. As well, they often turned to their family and friends when they encountered difficulties in settlement and needed help" (Longitudinal Survey of Immigrants to Canada 2001). These networks are key to the survival of newcomers because those from the newcomers' community may identify with the problems faced by the newcomer, as they might have been through it themselves. In fact, immigrants beyond those from an individual's boundary community may also be willing to help.

Many mainstream Canadians truly believe that they are wonderful people and many are. Most would agree that there is some racism in Canada but probably not admit to being racists themselves. But for the immigrant with a number of degrees under her belt and a track record of success who cannot get the time of day it takes a heavy purchase on faith to believe that all is well under the Canadian sun. As the number of immigrants increases, and some are able to attain a measure of success perhaps they will offer one another opportunities where those in the mainstream may not have come through. Just such a situation seems to have occurred in the case of Oved Tal, an Israeli native who started a company, Girit Projects, in Richmond Hill, Ontario. Many of the people working at Girit are recent immigrants from non-English speaking countries.

It may be that some Canadians equate having an accent with stupidity. It is well worth remembering that some of these immigrants speak three, four, or five languages and can read, write, and speak English perfectly, their accent notwith-standing. Meanwhile, not a few Canadians get into fits of apoplexy at the least bit of pressure to learn the other official language.

It's clear that there is hope even though perhaps Canada needs more people like Tal. Who knows? Perhaps, in the near future you will find yourself in a position where you can extend a helping hand to other immigrants. Canada is a great country but one has to wonder if this country could possibly not be even better were it to tap into the energies, skills, creativity, and talents of all immigrants – accent or no accent.

Business Immigrants: What's the Deal?

Many business immigrants who close down their business or quit their lucrative jobs for a chance at a whole new life in such coveted destinations as Canada become disappointed and disillusioned. For many business immigrants from Asia, coming to Canada means being able to live in a big house, have their children attend the best schools and even have the freedom of self-expression that they might not have had back home. Unfortunately, however, some of these immigrants end up losing their capital and source of income due mainly to high taxes, lack of appropriate business network, and inadequate niche markets for their businesses. Some of these business immigrants eventually fold their businesses and work for other businesses or go back to school to obtain Canadian educational qualifications in order to accumulate capital and experience to start niche businesses that thrive on ethnic markets.

Dealing with the Language Issue

Immigrants to Canada come with various levels of facility in the official languages of Canada. For those who come from countries such as the United Kingdom, Australia, or South Africa, there is usually no problem, as their accents are considered cute and thus desirable. It also helps that qualifications from these countries are often recognized in Canada. Organizations like SUCCESS in Vancouver; Victoria Immigrant and Refugee Centre (VIRC) and Inter-Cultural Association of Greater Victoria (ICA) (British Columbia), offer language programs that assist newcomers to integrate. Most major cities in Canada have similar organizations, or the high schools, colleges, or universities might have courses specifically geared towards English as a Foreign Language (EFL) or English as a Second Language (ESL) learners. The courses offered in these centres go beyond language to other elements such as résumé writing, income tax preparation, or even starting one's own business. One Korean immigrant in Vancouver who started an import-export business credits SUCCESS for the excellence of its business-training program which gave him the confidence to go ahead. Other courses that have benefited some immigrants include learning about Canada's banking system and how to purchase car insurance.

Need for Networking

Networking is one of the crucial strategic resources that facilitate the integration of immigrants, refugees and international students into the mainstream from the margins of Canadian society. But what exactly is networking? According to the report "Welcome to Canada: What You Should Know,"

> "Networking" is also a popular way of finding a job in Canada. This means contacting all the people you know, including your friends and relatives, and letting them know you are looking for work. This may help you to find a job that is not actually advertised anywhere. Job-finding clubs run by immigrant-serving organizations may also be useful. There are also private job placement agencies that may be able to help you find permanent, temporary or contract work. Remember that since employers pay a fee to use these agencies, your salary may be somewhat lower than it would be if you found the job by yourself. These agencies are listed in the yellow pages.
> (Welcome to Canada 2003 p. 27,
> http://www.cic.gc.ca/english/pdf/pub/welcome.pdf)

So, don't rely only on newspapers in your search for a job. Most city libraries carry books that list professional associations. Their websites or newsletters may carry a list of current openings. Even if one does not yet have a job in a professional field it might be possible to join first as an associate or under some such classification until one meets the other qualifications stipulated by the organization. Such organizations sometimes offer opportunities for volunteering, dinners, or other get-togethers, which can offer the chance to meet other people. Some of those you meet might, in the future, provide an entrée into a job but even if such networking does not lead to a job it may lead to better understanding between human beings who just happen to have been born and bred in different parts of the planet. And that too is good. Being involved in the organization can also allow you to exhibit some of your skills whether, in helping the association with organization of events or in some other area.

As a new entrant to Canada unless you are perceived to be someone of great means it is safe to say that you carry little influence. You may have a string of degrees to your name, managed to line up a million camels across the Sahara or single-handedly wrestled a dozen bulls to the ground. As an immigrant you start almost from zero. Statistics may indicate that immigrants are contributing mightily to the economy but for the average Canadian that may be a lot of hocus-pocus. You are in the country to "steal" jobs, not to create them, say those opposed to immigration. Why else are you sending out résumés at such a hot and heavy pace? Some Canadians may not see any real connection between their lives and yours except that you pose a threat to their jobs or those of their family members and friends. When you present your résumé and cover letter the manager or human resources personnel have no feeling of regret throwing them into the wastepaper basket. You are a nonentity. They do not know you and couldn't care less what you claim to have done in the past. But what if they knew you, not just as a stranger looking for a job but as a neighbour, a friend, or a member of their Rotary Club? Would that make a difference? In most cases the answer is yes.

Self-Employment

For immigrants with a record of success running businesses in their home country lack of access to the Canadian job market may provide the impetus to start their own business. While such individuals may have to acquaint themselves with the Canadian business environment there are indications that many immigrants have had a measure of success going this route. Those with strong community connections may find it a bit easier, however, considering that new immigrants may also meet with roadblocks when trying to borrow money from the bank. One population group in Canada that has found success in self-employment is the Koreans. Many have found profitable niches operating businesses such as convenience stores, coin laundries, or coffee shops. As self-employed individuals they do not have to deal with the problem of selling potential employers on their language skills and how this would affect their performance on the job. Having confidence in their abilities many find that despite their lack of perceived fluency in English this is hardly a big barrier in dealing with customers. The key point is that many Koreans have succeeded in the self-employment arena because of networking opportunities they enjoy in the Korean community. As Wong notes, "networking is another reason Koreans – and not other ethnic groups – have converged on convenience stores. Brother helps brother get started, cousin helps cousin, and everyone is bound together by language, culture and a vibrant community of churches" (Wong 2002).

Of course, such networking need not be only along the lines of race or culture. The success of Korean-Canadians in this area indicates that even in the face of seemingly insurmountable barriers, putting two, three, or four heads together can lead to success for the whole group where such success might have eluded individuals trying to make it on their own. In the absence of such networking opportunities you might have to go solo and do the research necessary to find out if you can make a go of one business or the other. There is no shortage of information in Canada and the United States on how to run every imaginable kind of business. You just have to make it your business to find out, and your local public library or the magazine racks of your neighbourhood bookstore may be good places to start.

Engineer and Hong Kong immigrant K.Y. Ho is one of many success stories where self-employment is concerned. Ho's company, ATI, of Markham, Ontario, founded in 1985, is in the business of making "graphics accelerator" chips as well as graphic expansion cards. Even though the computer graphics hardware industry is a highly competitive one, Ho and his associates have been able to pile success on top of success at every turn.

Another person who has found success in self-employment is Jerry Braganza, of Indian descent, who came to Canada about 30 years ago as a refugee from Uganda. He came with no money and found himself a job within a week. Braganza admits to having been lonely at first but he and his wife Rita now have a large circle of friends. Braganza is also no longer penniless as when he first arrived in Canada. His travel agency, which has five employees, brings in $3 million in sales every year (Janigan 2002). Can immigrants make a success of business in Canada? You better believe it.

You may be thinking so big as a potential entrepreneur that you may be ignoring an opportunity to start a business that could take you off the unemployment rolls. While we often hear or read about entrepreneurs doing millions of dollars in sales there are many others who make just about what they might make working for a company but without the hassle of a boss breathing down their necks. If you are unemployed and have a little bit of money to spare it may be a good idea to explore the possibility of starting a home-based business, one that will not require substantial investment in assets. You may already have a telephone, a fax, and a cell phone, along with expertise in some field such as accounting or editing. Rather than renting a place that might hang around your neck like an albatross you can simply work from home. In considering the opportunity, forget about those that require thousands of dollars to start, unless of course, you have a few million bucks stashed away. Especially with the Internet there are many businesses that are bringing in a tidy income, nothing like what Bill Gates makes certainly, but enough to ensure that you do not have to take a job that is far below your professional status or accomplishments.

Most people automatically assume that it is difficult to get into business. Even without the backing of any research they pronounce with authority that you need a permit to do this or that. In many cases, business permits are required but why not go down to the office in question and get that permit instead of just talking about it. In Canada, you can just walk into a provincial business registration office, do a name search, and register your business in a matter of minutes. So instead of assuming that what you want to do is impossibly difficult take the time to inquire and gain intimate knowledge of the business. It may not be as difficult as you suppose.

The Hidden Job Market

The newspapers may offer many job listings every day but this is often only a fraction of job openings available. In the newspaper field, for example, jobs are often advertised in the mainstream publications, meaning that people who confine themselves to ethnic magazines might not be exposed to the full range of opportunities. Gerry Nott, deputy editor of the Calgary Herald, believes that newspapers should not be trying to socially engineer the demographics of the newsroom but that job opportunities should be advertised as widely as possible. This suggests that rather than only going after jobs that are advertised, approach companies that one might wish to work for even when there is no advertisement for an opening. Your request may come at just the time when the company needs someone with your background and qualifications, or it could be that you would be placed on a waiting list for possible consideration in the near future. There are also suggestions in some quarters that by purposely reaching out to immigrants or people of colour employers are being forced to hire people who are less qualified. At the same time some immigrants and minorities are told that they are overqualified. In any case, new entrants to Canada need to appraise their qualifications fairly and to ensure that they have the skills or qualifications required and that these match the job. In some cases, this might mean performing surgery on your résumé and removing some sections that might signal that you are too qualified for a particular job.

Opportunities within the Ethnic Market

Some individuals have found opportunities not in seeking jobs within the mainstream but in serving their own and other ethnic communities. James Ho, a Taiwanese immigrant who owns Vancouver multicultural radio station CHMB, won through his company, Multivan Broadcasting Corporation, the rights to begin an ethnic television service in the Greater Vancouver area. The company's goal is to broadcast mainly to the Chinese and South Asian communities, which together number over half a million in the Lower Mainland. Even though Ho and his four partners competed against bigger fish such as the Toronto-based Rogers Group, they won the rights from the Canadian Radio-television and Tele-communications Commission (CRTC), much to their shock. If Ho and his partners had sat around talking about racism they might never have got to the point of submitting their application. Canada has a history of racism but the country is continually changing, led by government efforts to educate the population to the benefits of living in a multicultural environment. Some Canadians already perceive the advantage of this strategy; others are not so convinced and see it as a dilution of the traditional character of the nation. In response to a letter lambasting immigrants for drug dealing and drive-by shootings in Vancouver, Marta Goodwin (2003) noted the extent to which immigrants contribute to her lifestyle. Not only is her dentist an immigrant, so is her hairdresser. In addition, she has a secretary who is an immigrant and uses the services of a drycleaner who is an immigrant. Furthermore, her building manager and the contractor that she contracted to lay her floor tiles come from another country. She continues: "The guy who fixes my car is an immigrant. The woman who took my blood for testing last month was an immigrant... you can observe the number of kids from immigrant homes who are at the top of their classes in our high schools, who are receiving scholarships to colleges and universities, who are volunteering in their community, who are working after school in the family business or who are performing in the local arts scene" (Goodwin 2003).

Certainly, not all Canadians see immigrants with a jaundiced eye.

Employment Counselling

Canadian-born individuals who have been out of the work world for some time, due perhaps to raising a child, often find that they need to brush up on their knowledge of how to do a job search. Even though English or French is their mother tongue they go through mock interviews and seek help preparing their résumé. Others have found that they need to increase their familiarity with various computer programs or zero in on the use of specific programs that are relevant to their particular area of expertise. For example, a bookkeeper may be familiar with the manual system of accounting and have decades of experience. In Canada most companies are doing computer-based bookkeeping and accounting so without knowledge of various accounting software packages a person with only manual bookkeeping experience might find it difficult to get a job.

To help both immigrants and native-born Canadians almost every major city in Canada, and some smaller ones too, have employment counselling centres; the provincial or federal government may sponsor such programs, while others are private. In some counselling courses participants have practice runs and learn about when in the interview process, for example, they can expect to engage in small talk.

After all, it is not enough to be able to do one's job; colleagues have to be comfortable in dealing with you. Considering your "foreign" background Canadians are usually not sure if they will be able to converse freely with you, share jokes, and generally get along without any problems. Your serious demeanour may make your co-workers think that you are perpetually angry or that you have a chip on your shoulder. Remember that even native-born Canadians have to give an indication of being able to fit in with a particular organization otherwise they don't get hired. Such elements as body language and wardrobe, which immigrants might not have given much thought to, can loom large when one is looking for a job. For example, in some cultures, looking people in the eye is considered rude especially if one is communicating with someone older or in a position of authority. In Canada, however, an individual who is unable to meet an interviewer's gaze might be considered shifty or as someone who cannot be trusted or as one who has something to hide. Also, folding one's arms or crossing one's legs have meanings in Canadian culture that may be different from those in one's own culture. Without knowing the expectations in Canadian culture one risks sending out alienating signals to those in the mainstream.

Professional Jargon

Also, in some cases, the highly-skilled technical language of a profession may be an obstacle for an immigrant. Speaking everyday English is itself a challenge for some immigrants. Adding occupational jargon to the mix can make matters really complicated. While one could just buy a book and study the technical words it would probably please employers if you have taken a course in Canada that covers such jargon.

Frumpy, Dowdy, Go Away

While some immigrants have well-padded bank accounts others struggle from day to day. But going to a high-level job in your jeans or old pants may send the wrong message about you to potential recruiters. You should know the kind of dress code that is expected for people in your particular kind of work. Just as you might not find success wearing a $1,000 suit to a plumbing job interview, you might not cut it at an interview for public relations if you wear your frumpy old clothes. Polished shoes, the cut of your suit, the colour of your skirt, how much jewellery you wear – these are all elements that can affect whether you can get a job or not. And what may be perfectly acceptable in your home country may not be acceptable in Canada. You might argue that your shoe is not going to be doing the accounting or that your skirt has nothing to do with whether you can analyze financial statements. True, but this is the nature of the beast, and if you want to slay it you had better play by the rules.

Tailor Your Résumé to the Job

It's a good idea to tailor your résumé to particular jobs. From your master résumé you can retool your résumé to fit whatever particular employers are looking for. In order to do a proper job of tailoring your résumé you need to research the company to which you are applying or read with an eagle's eye their requirements for the job. Rather than presenting yourself as a generalist let the potential employer know that you have particular expertise that fits in with just what they are looking for. According to Carole Kanchier, a psychologist and author of *Dare to Change Your Job and Your Life*, there is a difference between those who usually succeed in clinching jobs, such as at job fairs and those who fail. Although Kanchier's advice is targeted towards those who seek jobs at job fairs there is much that can benefit job seekers in general. Kanchier found that unsuccessful candidates were generally unprepared and were without focus. Moreover, rather than specifying relevant skills they would ask for any kind of work. In effect, while companies are looking for specialists these individuals sell themselves as generalists, with little chance of success. Furthermore, those who dress casually look awkward or project an aura of defeat rarely succeed in clinching the job. Unsuccessful candidates, according to Kanchier, are usually inattentive when job descriptions are being provided and they often ask what employers expect of an ideal candidate, signalling right off the bat that they have no clue what is expected of them. Those who complain about their former companies or bosses are rarely successful in finding new jobs. And those who have only dollar signs in their eyes are shown the door as quickly as they come in. The story, however, is different for those who succeed in their job search efforts.

Successful candidates: Are prepared, direct, focused and have clear goals; dress professionally and act like they're in a real interview situation; come with several copies of an up-to-date résumé that has a clear career objective and summary of skills; are enthusiastic, optimistic, friendly, with a strong handshake; talk to many companies to get details and expand their job search. Successful candidates also: Ask key questions to learn about the company, jobs available and skills required; go away with several new contacts; keep an open mind about companies and opportunities; thank the interviewers for their time; follow up leads and contacts.

(Kanchier 2001)

Strategies for Successful Job Interviews

Being able to speak fluently does not guarantee that you'll ace any interview. Often to do well interview preparation is the key, which is why getting someone to ask you possible questions you might encounter at an interview and practicing your responses has been proven to be a good way for job seekers. Put some thought into your responses, ensuring that nothing will surprise you. If you are well prepared there's a good chance you will be able to cope even when you get a question that you were not expecting. To go unprepared is anathema.

At a Toastmasters public speaking meeting a blind Toastmaster from another club dazzled members of the host club by giving a superb "impromptu" speech on potatoes. One neophyte Toastmaster, clearly impressed, approached the master speaker after the meeting to inquire about the secret to how one could be so eloquent in an impromptu speech. The master said: "The key to giving a great speech is to have given it several times before." While to all of those in the room the presentation was a spontaneous outpouring of love, reverence, and praise upon the humble potato the master knew better. He had thought much about this topic and might have given variations of it at home or at his home club. By the time it was delivered with such masterly stroke the blind Toastmaster had had more than ample preparation. You can also dazzle an interviewer by doing a number of practice sessions. It is similar with magicians who dazzle their audiences with what seem like spontaneous acts; actually, those are often the result of much preparation. Ditto with street performers who test their lines on different audiences until they get the combination of comments and repartees that generate maximum entertainment value for the audience. Don't leave anything to chance.

The Screening Interview

One interview method that employers and recruiters use to save themselves much headache is the screening interview. You have sent in your résumé to a company. While you are waiting for them to write, you get a phone call with the caller requesting to ask you a few questions. You may be totally unprepared but this interview is no less important than one that may have occurred at the company's premises. With this kind of telephone interview if you do not do well you are not likely to see the company's lobby, period. When you are looking for a job you need to be prepared at all times then, as you do not know whether your interview will take place in person or on the phone. As Janis Foord Kirk, a career consultant and freelance columnist advises, "No matter what style of interview you find yourself in, accept that each has two different agendas. Interviewers represent employers. Their role is to question, probe, and to assess your suitability for the job. You, as a job seeker, have a couple of motives to discuss your background and skills and how they relate to the job in question and to find out all you can about the position, the department, the company" (Kirk 1992).

Body Language

Non-verbal cues communicate as surely as what comes out of the lips. In Canada, it is recommended that one make eye contact but one should be careful not to appear to be staring (Beauchesne 2004). Other suggestions include not invading the interviewer's space. In some cultures, it is acceptable to stand close, face to face with someone, as you talk. In Canada, leaning forward in your seat, a little too much, could make the interviewer uncomfortable. As Erich Beauchesne explains in the Vancouver Sun article, "Body Language Tells a Lot at Job Interviews," not only should you relax your face but also, too much nodding is bad though nodding to show understanding of a point is all right. Even though gestures are generally considered important one should not overuse them and neither should one tap fingers or feet as this gives the impression of being nervous. "During group interviews, common for executive-level candidates, try to make eye level with everyone there, regardless of who asks the question, to demonstrate your ability to handle group situations" (Beauchesne 2004).

A Community of Trust

Communities that have trust among themselves are able to get ahead much faster than those in which distrust abounds. In Belgium, Holland and other major diamond selling centres around the world millions of dollars in deals are done over a simple handshake. Why? Because the people involved in these transactions have established identities as people of integrity. Thus they entrust one another with more and more responsibility knowing that the outcome will be as expected – fair and without any underhandedness. It seems a bit unfair when minority communities riddled with distrust, unable to work with one another, expect those in the mainstream to embrace them and entrust them with important responsibilities. In effect, if your own family members are afraid to entrust you with responsibility and the rewards that go with it, why should strangers put their interests at risk dealing with you? It is said that several decades ago when one population group in the United States continually felt the sting of racism, being denied access to hotels, jobs, and other similar institutions and establishments, they pooled their funds together, and using intermediaries, bought as many hotels, motels, and resorts as possible. When people work together amicably and with trust they are able to solve problems on a larger scale than they might be able to do on an individual basis. The Chinese, for example, who have a long history of traveling and doing business abroad, have name associations and benevolent associations that help newcomers gain a foothold in their new society. They take this very seriously because they are aware that a negative image, even of one of their own, can reflect negatively on the whole group. Some in minority communities complain about the difficulty of obtaining loans from mainstream banking institutions. Now, have they considered opening their own bank or credit union? Difficult? Maybe, but if it were impossible, there would be no Khalsa Credit Union, a closed-bond credit union for the Sikh community.

CHAPTER SEVEN

MAKING CANADA YOUR HOME

Canada: Prospects and Perils

Canada, as one of the Pacific Rim nations, a neighbour of the United States and only a few hours' flight from Europe, is well positioned for the individual who has dreams of getting involved in international business. For some, however, dreams of international travel can wait. For now, the journey towards financial freedom, along with social equity, is of more pressing concern. Most have come to Canada with the full intention of staying. There is no Plan B.

Why You Should Feel at Home in Canada

The concept of multiculturalism, which allows Canadians to freely promote their individual cultures, is considered by some to be one of the strengths of Canada and one reason why immigrants should feel at home. In the article "Open the Gates Wide," Rudyard Griffiths opens a new and refreshing front on the debate on immigration. According to him, much of the debate has been framed in terms of the economic benefits that immigrants can bring to more established Canadians. This suggests that other than such potential economic benefits it is probably useless, even dangerous, to bring in large numbers of immigrants. Griffiths sees immigrants as the key to strengthening the identity of Canada rather than diluting it. Even though the federal government has been promoting multiculturalism for over 30 years not all Canadians are comfortable with it. They see the notion of hyphenated Canadians as not being positive for the identity of Canadians. While Canadians are willing to tolerate a measure of immigration because of the economic benefits, Griffiths argues that if Canadians were to take a closer look they would realize that despite coming from many different lands and speaking a multiplicity of tongues, immigrants strengthen the fabric of Canadian society in a number of deliberate and specific ways. Griffiths argues for a doubling of immigration, not on the basis of economic advantage but for the sake of preserving a "common set of Canadian values and way of life. In five years of exhaustive polling by my organization – the Dominion Institute, a history advocacy organization – the data has consistently shown that immigrants know more about Canada and Canadian history than natural-born citizens. That applies not only to knowledge of Canada's civic institutions and the way the government functions, but also to such issues as Confederation and the repatriation of the Constitution" (Griffiths 2002). Immigrants coming to Canada, argues Griffiths, come here based on a rational choice whereas those born in Canada often take the country for granted.

Even though not everyone is willing to lay down the red carpet for immigrants, in many areas of Canadian life, immigrants are very much a fact of life. Many formerly all-white enclaves have gradually become mixed communities and all without some of the race riots and disturbances that have rocked cities in America and the United Kingdom. Calgary high school principal Stephanie Davis may be on to something when she suggests that the myth of Canadian "niceness" may have created the reality of their welcoming attitude towards immigrants (Dyer 2001). In proportion to its population, Canada accepts "twice as many people as the United States and four times as many as the United Kingdom. What is truly remarkable is the ethnic profile of the immigrants to Canada, which is unique in how closely it matches the global distribution of the human population... Canada, more than anywhere else, is truly becoming the world in one country" (Dyer 2001). Welcome home.

Reach Out to Others

Some immigrants concede that Canadians are nice enough but they wonder why it is that they cannot form any strong bonds with Canadians. For Austin Clarke, now a famous and popular writer in Canada, the beginning of life in Canada was not easy. Having grown up in Barbados the move to Canada was a big change that pushed him off his moorings. By leaving Barbados he had left the only place he could truly call "home." In Clarke's early years in Canada he admitted that he could not pick one person with whom he was free to share confidences; he believed that a significant part of his history and development ended when he arrived in Toronto (Bethune 2003). For a while Clarke taught in the United States and even worked briefly in Barbados but returned again and again to Toronto.

After more than 30 years in Canada Clarke finally seems to have found his moorings. Having come to Canada in 1955, at the age of 19, he worked at a number of menial jobs such as night watchman for Columbia Records and seasonal postal worker. Having been educated in the most prestigious high school in Barbados, Harrison College, Clarke already knew how to turn a phrase. In 1959, he got a job as a reporter with the Timmins Daily News in Ontario and that is where Clarke's career as a writer really began. In the 1970s Clarke gained a measure of fame for writing about the lives of black immigrants in Toronto. Finally, in 2002, Clarke's writing contribution to Canadian literature was rewarded with Canada's highest literary prize, the $25,000 Giller Prize. At the award ceremony Clarke finally admitted: "'I feel that my feet are planted here in this landscape'... With the Giller, Clarke was able to feel that his love for Canada – "the best place in the world to live" – was fully reciprocated. It was one of the best moments in the life of Austin Clarke, a Canadian novelist. 'I feel there's such freshness in our writing, such a feeling that we can do anything at a time when there is great pride in being able to say, 'I'm a Canadian writer'" (Nurse 2003). Unlike Austin Clarke you may not have to wait for 30 years to feel at home in Canada. Godspeed.

Overcoming Feelings of Alienation in Your New Home

People who feel secure are better able to weather attacks on their identity. In a new country, the attack on your identity may be either direct or indirect. When someone calls you by an ethnic slur, that is a direct attack. But there are many areas where you will be denied or rejected without your knowing necessarily that it was because of your identity. Some in the mainstream culture feel that their majority position and the privilege that comes with it are under attack if a sizeable group of immigrants move in. Immigrants are also afraid of being constantly eclipsed by the established mainstream society. If both parties set aside their fears and make the project of getting to know the other a priority in their lives perhaps some of the problems and misunderstandings among different communities will be averted. In "Visible Majorities," Gwynne Dyer writes about an old friend of his, Ming, who has lived in Montreal since 1982. This brilliant watercolourist left Hong Kong at a time when family and friends could not appreciate the possibility of his making a career as a painter, and so Ming had to toil by day as a teacher and paint by night. In Canada, Ming met Guibert and the two have been together for over 16 years. "It's a very private relationship, but it's also a kind of paradigm of the new Canada: a French Canadian born in Sherbrooke living with a Chinese born in Hong Kong for whom English is a second language and French only a third. Guibert's children from an earlier marriage lived with them for years, as did one of Ming's young nephews from Hong Kong, and even the large extended families in Hong Kong and in Quebec are now part of the same web of relationships" (Dyer 2001). Can immigrants and Canadian-born learn to live with, laugh with, and love each other? Gwynne Dyer, for one, seems to think so. Dyer also believes that multiculturalism may have helped Canadians shift from the two great divides of English and French, something that might eventually have been the undoing of the country.

Forging Relationships

Forging relationships with people helps immigrants become a part of the fabric of Canadian society. There are many immigrants who live in Canada but do not feel themselves a part of the society. They have no real connections with people in the mainstream and therefore feel as though they were an island in the Canadian sea. If you want to succeed in Canada you need to forge relationships. This is because when you have connections with people, whether based on blood, friendship, or some mutual interests it is more difficult for them to turn you down when a need arises in your life. It is just human nature, truth that has continued down through the ages. As Professor Gavin Kennedy of Edinburgh Business School, an expert on negotiation and influence notes, "Relationships are barriers to defection, which is why influencing strategies aim to develop strong relationships with the implicit goal of preventing defections" (Kennedy 2000). There is another aspect to forming relationships. It allows people to get an idea of who you are as a person. They get to know your character and it is then much easier for them to commit to involving you in important areas of their life whether socially or in a business capacity. Of course, in a perfect world your résumé and background, along with an interview should be enough to get you a position for which you are qualified. As a new entrant, however, you may have to rely on more than your résumé and cover letter to vouch for you. People with whom you have formed a relationship will be able to serve as references for you. Incidentally, the Canadian system encourages such relationships. Whether you are applying for a job, a passport or a bank loan you require references, people who can vouch for your character. The more such people you have in your corner the easier your path towards success in Canadian society will be.

Engage with Canadians where they are most relaxed. This may be in the churches and the mosques and the temples and the synagogues and the hockey rinks, business conventions, workshops, charity events, festivals, and theatrical performances. The rodeo and flea markets also come to mind. Friendship, however, cannot be forced. Allow your personality to shine through and you may be able to draw people into your circle. Seeking friends and allies in your host country is also a numbers game. Not everyone you meet will be enamoured of you and want you for a friend but chances are the more people you meet and greet the better the chances that some of them will find in you a kindred spirit.

Immigrants who are into ice hockey and baseball, watch all the games, and master the lingo, usually have no problem fitting into Canadian society. Most Canucks can talk the language of hockey. But, of course, the range of interests of Canadians is wide and as long as you are holed up at home there is not much chance that you will be able to forge the kind of relationships that will allow you to enhance other people's lives while perhaps also benefiting from the human interaction. Immigrants who make Canadian friends are in a far better position to enjoy their experience of living in Canada compared to those who stick only with those from their national, religious, or ethnic background. As a new immigrant you have a need to influence those around you. You do not have the power to make anyone do your bidding but by deploying some influencing strategies you will be able to bring some people on your side and help accelerate your program of adaptation to Canadian life. As defined in the book *Influence*, by Gavin Kennedy (2000), "Influencing is the process by which we obtain what we want by affecting the thoughts, feelings and behaviours of others who are able to make decisions that affect ourselves and over whom we may have limited or no formal authority." Most immigrants might want to have friends and associates that cut across their boundary community. Lack of such interaction may lead to the feeling that Canada offers an inferior version of the rich social connections that they might have enjoyed in their home countries. After all, in Canada the number of people who speak your language and are known to you may be much smaller compared to the social network you may have built in your home country. Thus, if you are stuck with only interacting with people from your boundary community then would you not be better off going back home where you can enjoy similar relationships drawn from a much, much larger pool? What's the point of living in a foreign land if you do not care about knowing the people there? Some of the Hong Kong immigrants living in ethnic enclaves such as Richmond may come across as not wanting to associate with people from the mainstream (Chugani 1998) but such lack of cross-cultural association seems to make the experience of living in Canada less than satisfying. As one Hong Kong emigrant, a Toronto-based sociologist points out, "the failure to interact with mainstream society was one reason why many [from Hong Kong] wanted to go back" (Chugani 1998).

Gaining a Social Foothold Through Influence

The importance of deploying influencing strategies becomes clear when one considers that while immigrants may obtain jobs, they hardly ever make it to the upper echelons within the companies where they are employed. Even though it is taken for granted that this is mainly because of racism a closer look might reveal that there are some immigrants who have been able to win positions of leadership in their organizations. How come they were not snared by the net of racism? Could it be that these immigrants and visible minorities who are able to move up may be making use of skills that other immigrants may not have?

Influencing, by the way, requires a sustained effort. Trying to influence others requires taking the long-range view. You also need to listen to what others have to say. You are unlikely to do much influencing if you are the one who always does the talking. Sometimes, you have to keep quiet and listen to what others have to say. In Canada, people often deepen their relationships by participating in activities together. In some other countries, exchange of visits and long chats are the key to forging strong relationships. While in some countries acquaintances can visit family and friends unannounced, this is usually not the norm in Canada. A phone call will help establish if people have the time to meet and this may not even be in their home. You may meet people in coffee shops, restaurants, or perhaps even a park until the relationship has progressed and there is a bit of mutual trust established. Many immigrants have had to adapt to this norm and would not be pleased if you just showed up at their door unannounced. As with most things, however, personal discretion rather than rigid rules, may be your best guide.

The Pull Behaviour Type

Most relationships go through the so-called **fishing** stage. This is when newly acquainted individuals fish for information about each other. This may include asking each other's names, perhaps occupational affiliation, and other background information. It is possible that the conversation might not progress beyond this stage because one or the other loses interest in fishing for further details. When influencers make the acquaintance of strangers they do not allow the relationship to remain distant. They show interest in other people and do their best to establish connections that would move the relationship to a deeper level. "Fishing for common ground is the first step in a relationship, which, once found, is explored. Beware, though of the error of interrogating someone desperately and intensely from the moment of the first handshake or bow. People resent over-familiarity on a first meeting and they are cautious about going into too much detail about their personal circumstances" (Kennedy 2000). The second stage is the **enthusing** stage. In this stage you encourage an individual to enthuse about something of interest. It may be their accomplishments or experiences such as a trip to Nepal, first year in medical school, or their last bungee jump. Show interest in their story and you lay the foundation for a friendship that may last over many moons if not a lifetime. "By respectfully encouraging their enthusiasms you reinforce their positive feelings. To succeed in enthusing you had best convey a sense of your excitement in your manner. An emotionless tone does not energize those you wish to enthuse" (Kennedy 2000).

Wallowing, the next stage of the pull behaviour type is defined as the "empathetic probing of incidents, problems, moods and doubts. Wallowing encourages the other party to share more details about an event and allows you to empathize by showing that you understand the person's feelings" (Kennedy 2000). You also allow the other person to get something off his or her chest and shows that you are a concerned person, or at least, a good listener. In the book, *Making Major Sales* by Neil Rakham (Gover, Aldershot, 1987; cited in Kennedy 2000) an in-depth research on the sales process is presented. According to Rakham, good sales people do not jump in to try to solve a prospect's problems. "They note the opening they get from your having a problem, but they also encourage you to elaborate (i.e., wallow) on the wider consequences of your problem... Sharing those memories and feelings strengthen relationships in an influencing sequence" (Kennedy 2000). The final step is **revealing**. Most of your contacts may not have progressed to the revealing stage especially if you are new to a country. Beyond the short biography, of name, place of birth, and perhaps religious affiliation or the lack thereof, revealing goes a little further. People in a relationship share with each other tidbits about their lives as well as feelings, expectations, dreams, and hopes. In addition, "Details of who they are, where they come from, current domestic arrangements, current job circumstances, their sexual preferences and so on are exchanged, and each lets the other enter her private territory in reciprocation for being allowed into the other's private territory" (Kennedy 2000). When someone shows an interest in learning more about you to a greater extent beyond the fishing state it would be appropriate to give them a chance to also share some information either around the same time or later. One-sided revelation will send a message that you're not interested in them, which may also curtail the interest they had shown in you.

The Push Behaviour Type

The so-called push strategy works better where there is already an established relationship, a robust one, otherwise they can rupture a fragile relationship. The first of the push behaviours is **reasoning**. "Rational reasoning is highly regarded in the West, where there is a strong prejudice in favour of rationality in managerial theory. In argumentative discourse, logic is assumed to be superior to subjectivism. From a given premise a logical conclusion follows. Another conclusion is false and logical implication should be rejected" (Kennedy 2000). Making **suggestions** also contributes to building a relationship. If you give someone good advice based on your knowledge or expertise that person is unlikely to ignore you the next time he or she sees you. Next is **asserting**, which is much stronger and assumes a closer relationship in the first place.

Coercive behaviour, the most extreme in influencing relationships, can be effective in relationships that are already strong. If not used with care, however, they can backfire and lead to the opposite outcome. Some people react to coercion by not doing what is expected of them.

> The use of coercion rather than the softer influence behaviours indicates some form of power over the target. Relationships give power to the influencer and, ironically, partners behave towards each other in ways that would not be tolerated if there were no relationship. Examples of altercations between domestic partners come to mind (it has been observed that spouses treat each other much worse than they treat their lovers), as do interpersonal tensions between politicians in the same party (some cannot bear to be in the same room as fellow members).
>
> (Kennedy 2000)

The new entrant to Canada will find occasion to use almost the full range of influencing behaviours. Because of the possibly stronger relationship between the immigrant and those in the person's boundary community some of the push behaviours might work better with those in the boundary community whose greater knowledge of Canada may be enlisted from time to time as the immigrant takes the first tentative steps towards entry into mainstream Canadian society. Because your relationship with your family and friends is more robust you can push them more. On the other hand, you cannot push someone you have just met; pull behaviours work better for new acquaintances.

Be Sociable

A person who is perceived to be sociable, willing to converse, play or share in activities with others is usually better received than the individual who always hangs back. Go through newspaper accounts of rapists, murderers and various assorted psychopaths and you will find that invariably the perpetrator is said to have been a loner. This may be a stereotype but you can readily appreciate how ordinary Canadians can be nervous about seeing you go back and forth each day without friends of any sort. You may be spending most of your time among the dusty shelves of your local university library but your neighbours, of course, do not know that and may wonder if you have a dark side, which is why you are always just by yourself. The point here is that it is important to be informed and guard against behaviours that might unfairly pigeonhole you and hamper your progress in your new community.

Reciprocation

Doing good turns for others is its own reward. While you may not do good turns with the view to getting an express reward from others, reciprocation has a long history in human relations. A young boy develops a reputation in his neighbourhood as the kid who clears the snow off the front porch of his house and those of his closest neighbours. He helps the elderly lady living across the street whenever he can. He does not ask for payment when he does errands for the neighbours. If this boy should get into any kind of trouble, such as being hit by a motorbike, how do you think the neighbours would react? This boy has traded some influencing currencies with the people around him, which is why they will do all they can to help him in his time of need.

Most people do not know the glorious history of Ethiopia and only know the country from the pictures of emaciated men, women and children that splashed across television screens during the mid-1980s. Owing to years of drought and civil war there was a huge famine that propelled the world to respond with various fundraisers. Ethiopians were dying in huge numbers. As the aid poured in from all over the world a curious thing happened. The Ethiopian Red Cross sent $5,000 to Mexico City. Some who read about this news item were perplexed and assumed that it was an error. Ethiopia had sent $5,000 to Mexico City? No. But why would Ethiopians, in the midst of their suffering, send to Mexico money that they might have used to save a few of their own? Robert B. Cialdini, Regents' Professor of Psychology at Arizona State University in Tempe, was one of those who could not believe his eyes when he happened upon that news item. He made it a point to find out what was behind this incredible story. As it turns out the money had been sent to help earthquake victims in Mexico City. "Despite the enormous needs prevailing in Ethiopia, the money was being sent because Mexico had sent aid to Ethiopia in 1935, when it was invaded by Italy. So informed, I remained awed, but I was no longer puzzled. The need to reciprocate had transcended great cultural differences, long distances, acute famine, and immediate self-interest. Quite simply, a half-century later, against all countervailing forces, obligation triumphed" (Cialdini 1993). What obligations do Canadians have to assist you? For Canadians' own self-interest it would be a good idea to smooth the path for immigrants so that they can contribute their energies and their taxes to the building up of the country. Most average Canadians do not necessarily share the enthusiasm of the government to bring in people from other parts of the world, in particular, visible minorities. For such individuals, there is no sense of obligation to immigrants, unless of course, you can create an obligation on their part by first trading in some influencing currencies.

All human societies go by the rule of reciprocity. From being a faceless immigrant you would take on more colour and importance among those around you if you extend yourself and assist others. To paraphrase J. F. Kennedy, think not what Canada or your community can do for you but what you can do for your community and for Canada. According to Cialdini, "The impressive aspect of the rule of reciprocation and the sense of obligation that goes with it is its pervasiveness in human culture. The noted archaeologist Richard Leakey ascribes the essence of what makes us human to the reciprocity system: We are human because our ancestors learned to share their food and their skills in an honoured network of obligation" (Cialdini 1993). If you want to become a true part of Canadian society you do not have to wait to be called upon before inserting yourself into the life of your community. As you do good turns for others you will feel rewarded for your selflessness. The rule of reciprocation, however, guarantees that some of those that you touch with your good works will feel obligated to lend you a helping hand when you most need it. It may be nothing more than a character reference, a job lead, or a partnership that starts you on the road to self-sufficiency and even prosperity.

Influencing Currencies

Doing good turns for others is one of the best ways to weave yourself into the seams of a new community. By doing good turns for others you may be saving your own life. How? The old saying, "One good turn deserves another," is the principle here. You never know when you might have to count on the goodwill of someone to whom you had done a selfless act. On the other hand, when you are mean to others, in your time of need they might not so willingly respond to your cries for help. The rule of reciprocity suggests that if others do a good turn for you "then they deserve to receive a comparable good turn from you" (Kennedy 2000). Examples of good turns that Professor Kennedy mentions in the book *Influence* include giving others a lift, working another's inconvenient shift, delivering a message, giving up a place in a queue, and swapping a shift or holiday. This is just a small sampling of good turns you can do for people around you. Even doing a good turn for a stranger is not a waste. Doing good turns with the expectation that you will receive a good turn, however, may be missing the point. Most good turns, "like romantic love, are often unrequited" (Kennedy 2000). If you want to be a member of the community in which you live, if you want to participate in the everyday life of Canadians you cannot always think of what you can get from the society. Some immigrants have found volunteering to be a worthwhile way to contribute to their local communities while also learning about expectations, norms, and mores of Canadian society. This acquired knowledge can subsequently make it easier for them to navigate their way through Canadian society.

A Story of Hope: The Daniel Igali Story

Daniel Igali was a member of the Nigerian wrestling team that participated in the Commonwealth Games in Victoria, B.C., in 1994. Rather than return to Nigeria where his dreams of wrestling glory might have gone up in smoke he decided to apply for refugee status and remain in Canada. Today, he is a Canadian hero, having won a gold medal for Canada in the 2000 Sydney, Australia Olympics. The road has not been easy for Igali but throughout his struggle there have been Canadians who have been willing to lend a helping hand. When, for example, Igali made the decision to stay in Canada, volunteer Tom Murphy, and his family took Igali in and assisted him with the application procedure. Another Canadian who did her best to make Igali feel at home was Maureen Methany whom he met through an acquaintance. In terms of professional sports opportunity, Satnam Johal of Surrey, British Columbia, a businessman who owns Spartan gave free room and board as well as training facilities to Daniel (Schuyler 2001). Mr. Igali soon started out as a part of the Simon Fraser University wrestling team. After one gruelling competition, the truth in the words of his coach that he may not believe in himself seems to have made an impression on the young man. This was during a Simon Fraser University tournament where he had the chance to wrestle with some of the top wrestlers from around the world. Whether in terms of his training or his education Igali got some help from Canadians who were eager to see him succeed. Today, with more of such help from Canadians he is moving steadily towards his goal of raising money to build a school in his hometown. Now, your talent may not lie in wrestling but you may have to find a way of connecting with ordinary Canadians who may yet help you wrestle your problems to the ground.

Make an Effort to Connect with Others

It is unfair to take Canadians' hesitancy in approaching you as a sign of mean-spiritedness. Some are simply shy or are not sure how to relate to you because of your "different" background. But rather than expecting your hosts to come to you why not show some friendliness to Canadians of every stripe. After all, building a relationship is hardly a one-way process. Some individuals may hesitate to approach you or embrace you not because they do not like you but because they are not comfortable with you. Now, don't get angry just yet. Think about it. Are you always comfortable approaching people you do not know? You will find that Canadians who have traveled outside the borders and explored other parts of the world might find it much easier to talk with "foreigners" – that is, immigrants. Human interaction is fraught with both opportunity and danger. Take a chance on your fellow Canadians. If you are not yet a Canadian citizen you soon will be. Why wait? Why not build bridges of friendship and trust from day one? "Where are you originally from?" is a question many immigrants have to answer as long as they live in Canada. To some immigrants, this is a loaded question, a prelude to the unleashing of the full force of prejudice. This may very well be so, but it may also be a question of curiosity. In any case, being overly sensitive is not likely to help build better and stronger relationships. Despite the differences in culture and worldviews there is still more that unites immigrants and the Canadian-born than meets the eye but both need to make an effort to find out. Immigrants want an opportunity to make their dreams come true in the same way that Canadian-born individuals want to succeed – in their careers, their home life and in their communities. If we make an effort to seek common ground there would be no need to worry that our differences would lead to problems. On the other hand, in a nation where all are peace loving our differences can be a cause for great celebration. Won't you bring out the bubbly?

Bridging the Gap: On a Personal Level

Immigrants should do their part towards the process of integration and mutual understanding. This means encountering everyday Canadians in different settings where there can be interaction. Parents who get involved in Parent-Teacher Association meetings have an opportunity to learn from their Canadian counterparts while also sharing with others their worldview. But where are Canadians to be found? Some immigrants and students who come to Canada to study English or French often lament the ease with which they are able to meet other immigrants and foreigners as opposed to native-born Canadians. Starting with one's own areas of interest, it is possible to meet Canadians who share those same interests. For example, if you are interested in crafts and like to visit craft fairs, it is possible to meet others with whom one has a common reference point from which friendship can blossom. Art shows, museum visits, hockey games, the rodeo, and even an evening at the theatre could all be starting points for forging friendships that may last a lifetime. Because immigrants' own interests might differ considerably from those of the Canadian-born, it might be necessary for immigrants who really want to understand Canadian culture to extend their primary areas of interest. Many Canadians have also shown an interest in learning more about other cultures, sometimes serving as eager patrons of the diverse offerings from the various ethnic communities in the country whether in terms of food, entertainment, or other aspects of culture.

Overcoming Isolation and Boredom

Some astronaut wives may return again and again from orbit to reconnect with their husbands while their children remain in Canada. Even though some in the media have accused some of the wealthier immigrants from Asia as having no intentions to develop roots in Canada the media forgets that the immigrants' children quickly adapt and adopt some Canadian values. For some of these families the acquisition of English language skills is considered very important for the children, along with Canada's education system, which encourages students to think rather than do rote memorization. Some children who are unable to cope with the highly competitive educational system in their home countries find in Canada a haven for the exploration of what they truly want to do with their lives. In fact, some of the young people from fast-paced centres in Asia such as Hong Kong and Taiwan prefer the relatively laidback lifestyle in Canada. Though the parents may sometimes see this as negative for their children, according to Johanna Waters' research, some of the astronaut wives admit that Canada offers them and their children an opportunity to develop other aspects of their personality.

For astronaut wives the first few months in Canada can be one of isolation and boredom. Some of these women might have had high-powered jobs in their home country but unemployed in Canada some are, initially, at a loss as to how to spend their time. In time, some have sought to connect with those in the mainstream. For example, in 1992, Claire came to Canada from Taiwan, intent on mastering English. She did not reach her goals simply by attending classes. Rather, she found success in an unlikely source, the local swimming pool "...where she met 'retired people' who were 'more willing to... help you.' In the sauna men would chat... and of course men like to talk about politicians, you know, current issues... And that's the way [I learned English]" (Waters 2003).

Most of the subjects of Waters' study attended English classes and were eager to learn the language. "Attending classes was one way in which women gained confidence while expanding their social networks. Many became particularly adept at integrating childcare and personal activities" (Waters 2003). Some also took an interest in reading about Canadian life and culture in order to gain greater insight into life in their new home. Some who went to school and took classes with Caucasians in subjects such as ceramics thought that but for their limited English they would have been able to forge stronger relationships with their Caucasian counterparts. Volunteering and the taking up of hobbies such as "quilting, pottery, dance, aerobics, computers, tennis, reading and sculpture, most of which revolved around the local community centre" (Waters 2003) helped to fill the void in their lives. For some, especially those who do not have to contend with the job search process and its dispiriting effect, living in Canada can indeed be the paradise that they had imagined it to be. "For Rose, moving away from the extended family in Taiwan has had a significant impact on her sense of freedom. As she explained: 'Now I am in Canada I am very happy! I can go anywhere! [laughs]… I can visit my friends. When they [the children] go to school I have my free time… So I enjoy Canadian life. [laughs]'" (Waters 2003).

In fact, rather than seeing the time spent in Canada as just biding their time to return to better things in their home countries, many of the astronaut wives in Waters' study got involved in their new community through volunteering as well as participation in sports and crafts. Also, "Learning English, so they could engage in meaningful conversation with local 'Caucasians' was top priority" (Waters 2003).

Of Fitness Centres, Hockey Rinks, and Mickey Mouse

One immigrant from Ethiopia found it virtually impossible to communicate with the Canadians with whom he worked in a restaurant. Even though many of the workers were high school and university students, their subject of conversation never strayed far from topics such as hockey, working out (body building), and cartoons. According to this immigrant, even though he sat with his newfound friends for hours on end, there were times when he could not contribute anything to the conversation. His areas of interest included politics and world history. Another immigrant from Iran, with a master's degree in biology, lamented why she was never able to meet Canadians who would engage her in intellectual discourse. For an immigrant, especially one who has to accept a job that puts bread on the table, seeking fellow intellectuals, may not be easy. Your path and that of the intellectuals diverge every morning as you head towards your bakery job and they to their… well, intellectual jobs. But consider that many universities hold free lectures to which the public is invited. Could that be a starting point for finding people with whom you can discuss the nuances in the thought patterns of Rousseau and Kierkegaard?

Taekwondo and *Tai Chi* clubs, bird watching clubs, camping and public speaking clubs all offer opportunities to meet Canadians with roots that go farther than one's own. Cultivating new interests may offer the potential for enlarging one's circle of friends. For example, a cricket-playing immigrant might not find many who share the love of cricket but might be able to build a new set of friendships around baseball. So the question is: do you really want to make friends or are you comfortable remaining within your current social or ethnic sphere? Think about the opportunities for mutual understanding that can arise when you GOYA[1] or GOTT[2]!

Be Aware of Local Customs

Some customs and holidays that might be meaningful to long-time Canadians may be completely new to immigrants. Holidays such as Halloween afford opportunities for building new friendships and for immigrants to demonstrate that they are willing to share in the spirit of camaraderie that the holiday engenders. For those who, because of religious or other reasons, may balk at participating, these holidays afford still more the opportunity to hold discussions. Delving into the origins of various holidays may lead to discussions that might take more than a few encounters to fully consider. Also, people are often more relaxed during such holidays as Christmas, Easter, Halloween, with each seasonal theme itself affording opportunities for conversation. Such efforts at reaching out to those in the mainstream also help to debunk the impression that some immigrants do not want to integrate but rather find comfort in operating within their own narrow boundary community.

Dig Our Scar First

Immigrants often come to Canada with high expectations not only of the potential economic success they will enjoy but also the expectation of almost perfect social interaction. This might have been encouraged by the image often portrayed in the media of "nice Canadians." Without suggesting that Canadians are not nice, immigrants might find it shocking, especially after living in Canada for a while, to find themselves repeatedly rejected for jobs for which they may be qualified. Under such circumstances, the immigrant, disillusioned by what might seem like petty-mindedness or constant carping by Canadians, might easily come to think of occupying the higher ground in terms of values. When racist graffiti was spray-painted on about twenty cars in downtown Vancouver in 1995, these activities were roundly condemned. But some members of the Chinese community took the opportunity to take a critical look at some of their own customs. In the spirit of self-criticism that ensued in the wake of the racist acts, *Ming Pao* published an informal poll in August of 1995 in which the Chinese leaders and the editorial made suggestions on proper conduct to members of the Chinese community. Chinese were advised to "avoid speaking Chinese loudly in mixed-language settings, avoid picking

---

[1] Get Off Your Ass (Kennedy 2000)
[2] Get On The Telephone (Kennedy 2000)

ears or cutting nails in public, practice caution before chopping down trees, avoid building a big house or buying a fancy car to flaunt wealth, stop squeezing fruit and vegetables too much at stores, refrain from blocking traffic while waiting to park and respect line-ups at counters" (Todd 1995). As well *Ming Pao* published an informal poll in which 57 per cent of the Chinese people who participated admitted that they might have inadvertently discriminated against a person from another race. Immigrants are rightly sensitive when they are discriminated against but as an immigrant do you also find yourself discriminating against others on the basis of their race, gender, national origin, creed, or some other criteria? Some immigrants have found their nemeses to be other immigrants who may have preceded them by a few years or an ancestor or two. From their more comfortable perch within Canadian society these more entrenched immigrants can also make life a living hell for newcomers. It would be naïve, therefore, to assume that when one refers to mainstream Canadian society it refers only to people of one colour or heritage.

Down but Not Out

It is quite revealing and somewhat disconcerting to see on Canadian streets, particularly in the major urban centres, people who appear to be down on their luck, sometimes with palms outstretched looking for a handout. Some immigrants may feel a sense of shame to expose their destitution so openly. The combination of factors that could lead to such an outcome may vary from person to person but the reality is that it could happen and has happened to people who never envisioned that they would ever find themselves in such a position. Sometimes, it may simply be because of a lack of information, as was the case with an immigrant who was not aware of his entitlement to Unemployment Insurance (now Employment Insurance) following a layoff from work. He spent several nights in city parks (a dangerous proposition) and in twenty-four hour coffee shops where he unsuccessfully tried night after night not to nod off. Meanwhile he tried to get another job, which under the circumstances was anything but easy.

Rather than give in to panhandling or worse, stealing, one should be aware that there are agencies all over the country that offer temporary respite from the occasional downturns of the economy or personal fortune.

You've Probably Had Your Moments

Even within a system with so many constraints for immigrants, if you are honest, you will admit you've had some great moments. Of course, you should not accept the crumbs and imagine that they are the whole loaf but it helps to take an objective look at one's life from time to time. If you've not yet had any great moments and opportunities in Canada, don't worry, you will, and when you do, just don't drop the ball.

If you've been around for a while, however, though you complain about not being able to get a loan remember there was a time when your credit was good and you could get a loan if you had had the need. But then you were flush with cash and in your eagerness to accumulate material things you began a buying binge – on credit. Not long after, you lost your job, making it difficult to pay off the credit cards. And with a bad credit rating things just spiralled out of control. Oh, you've had your moments.

Remember those one to five-hour long distance telephone calls you used to make? And let's not forget the collect calls that you used to accept day and night. Now, you've wised up so you quietly hang up the phone when any such calls come in. You are no fool. You tried to pay the phone company, but God, the phone bill was huge, all those long distance calls and you didn't make them all. Friends called from your house and you were too nice to tell them not to do so. But now you're carrying the bill on your head. The phone companies are relentless; they won't give you a break but if you'll be fair you will recall that you got ample warning, which you ignored. You needed to keep in touch with friends and family. But strangely enough, now that your phone line is disconnected, you don't miss those juicy conversations. You've had your moments.

And let's not forget that "beaut" you used to drive. Was it a Honda or a Toyota? It might even have been a large American car, a gas-guzzler. There was a time when you were working two jobs and had hardly any time for yourself. As a result you accumulated quite a bit of money in your account. The day you saw your multiple-page bank statement, you were so pleased. You had never had so much money in your life. This called for a bit of shopping; after all, you had been working hard. And so you went to that dealership on the outskirts of the city, the one that had rows and rows of cars, new and used. Of course, you didn't pay for the slightly used car in cash but you plunked down enough to reduce your monthly payments. Smart. But then you had to buy gas and let's not forget the insurance, either. Your friends were impressed. But that was before you were laid off from work. What a bummer. You still had to make the payments on the car. What seemed like a lot of money in your account now seemed to be dwindling fast and you couldn't get another job. You negotiated with the car dealership to stretch your payments a little farther, which meant in the end paying more than you expected. Tomorrow would be a good day, you thought.

Now, with so much time on your hands, watching Oprah and assorted soap operas, has become a way of life. You don't seem to mind the rest thanks to your Employment Insurance cheques. It was when you were watching Doctor Phil that your hand bumped a stack beside the sofa. This huge stack of Western Union receipts; you had forgotten all about them. These were the receipts of money you've sent home over the years. The folks back home say you're stingy. You never send them anything. Grabbing your Casio calculator you spent all day calculating money you've sent home all these years. "Oh, my Gosh, I've done quite a bit," you told yourself. You wondered if all that money could have gone into a down payment for a condo or a house; you wondered how big your RRSP (Registered Retirement Savings Plan) would be by now if you had put all that money away. Your folks consider you a total failure for not continuing to send them money. In your own eyes you could have done a little better; okay, a lot better. Yes, there is racism in Canada but if you'll be honest with yourself, you'll also admit that you've had your moments. You've met some wonderful people and because things are not so rosy right now it's easier to remember the people who crossed you the wrong way. You've had your moments, and Canada, thank God, remains a wonderful place. Just watch the quality of your decisions because in this great country you might just have a second chance. Don't blow it when you do.

There is Hope

It is important to remember that you have come to Canada at a time when the society is getting more and more used to the idea of multiculturalism. If you had come to Canada in the 1900s you might have had to contend with more blatant forms of racism. As Vic Satzewich (2004) writes in *Canadian Dimension*, "Decision makers and power holders within organizations still discriminate and treat individuals unequally. Further, organizations may still engage in systemic discrimination, as the debate about racial profiling within police forces suggest. However, there are few cases where discrimination and unequal treatment is formally endorsed in the laws of the land." Over the years, the Canadian government has introduced a number of legal prohibitions against discrimination. Because there is a mechanism for aggrieved parties to seek redress, people who might have discriminated with impunity in the past are now more likely to act with caution. This hardly means that discrimination has been stamped out but the country is making all attempts to, if not eliminate racism, at least reduce it. There was a time in Canada when there was legislated preference for whites in the country's immigration policy. Satzewich notes that "There are still racist remnants to immigration policy and practices, and certain policies impact immigrants and potential immigrants in different ways, but they are a far cry from the early 1960s, when race, colour, nationality, and a variety of euphemisms for "race" played a determining role in who got in." If you are not of European ancestry, the fact that you are in Canada, whether as an immigrant, refugee, or international student, speaks volumes about the more open attitude in Canada in recent years. According to Satzewich, "Some individuals still think racist thoughts, say racist things, treat people badly and deny jobs, promotions, housing and other resources to people because of the colour of their skin. In other words, there are still many ways in which opportunities, status and identities in Canada are degraded because of racism. There will never be a point where racial degradations do not happen. But it has become more difficult for individuals and organizations to say and do racist things without social opprobrium."

Life for many immigrants in Canada is not a cakewalk but few would trade it for the life they had back home. This is particularly so for those whose countries are in wretched circumstances, economically or politically. Much needs to be done in Canada for immigrants to feel at home but for those who put matters in proper perspective the current hardships may be a little easier to bear. Jan Wong, writer for the *Globe and Mail*, in a piece entitled "A Country of Sales Clerks," writes about a Korean family, the Bangs, who have found Canada to be more than an acceptable haven. Mr. Bang, a former pharmaceutical company sales manager moved to Canada because he could not see much advancement for himself in that job. Along with his nurse wife and their two children the family moved to Toronto where the parents work very long hours. Even so, they own the $185,000 two-storey building in which their store is located. Their two children have made it to university and Mr. Bang has been able to progress in his studies at the Royal Conservatory of Music to the point where he is able to teach others in the neighbourhood for $15 per half-hour. The Bangs are not millionaires and would probably be happier if they were in a much better financial position. Still, Mr. Bang, who became a Canadian citizen in 1994, says: "In Canada, if you want to do something, you do it. You're free. In Korea, you have to check with everybody's feelings, check your manager's face first" (Wong 2002).

CHAPTER EIGHT

WHY YOU SHOULD KEEP YOUR CHIN UP

Government Efforts

The complaints of immigrants regarding lack of recognition for their credentials are reaching the highest echelons of power in Canada. Thus, the government, along with academic institutions and regulatory bodies, has begun taking steps to rectify this situation. All over the country, from Newfoundland in the east to British Columbia in the west, Canadians are creating programs that will allow immigrants to fully contribute. In Quebec, for example, the Centre Génération Emploi, has created an intensive 8-week program, not to help immigrants flip burgers, but to help them access some of the higher level jobs they may have trained for. The program is financed by Emploi Quebec and the Quebec branch of IBM, which provided the space and the equipment. Believe it or not, this centre has been around for about twenty years, highlighting how important it is to seek out information. The program helps immigrants do a skills inventory and set up a portfolio of their accomplishments. This makes the participants better organized when they have to talk with potential employers; they can better communicate their strengths and expertise in a way that will be readily understood by Canadian business people. Many large corporations contact the centre for potential employees as they realize the truth in the notion that diversity is strength.

Credential Evaluation Services

Academic recognition services such as World Education Service provide evaluation services and verification of credentials (see Reminders and Resources section). The services of such companies help translate foreign credentials into their Canadian equivalents, thus easing the minds of employers regarding potential employees from outside of Canada. The Canadian Council for Human Resources in the Environment Industry (CCHREI) is one organization that is at the forefront of such efforts. Some employers in the environmental field who have taken a chance on those with foreign credentials have recognized that they didn't take a gamble at all. "Of course, this recruitment success is not so surprising when one considers that 93% of foreign practitioners seeking environmental employment (through CCHREI's EnviroJob Board) already have post-secondary education and experience in a number of environment-related fields" (Stevens 2004). Among efforts by CCHREI on foreign credential recognition is a proposal to set up a Strategic Immigration Electronic

Screening Plan. This plan aims to use the current National Occupational Standards (NOS) for environmental employment to set up a database of immigrants who have demonstrated experience in the environmental field. This would include recognition of experience outside of Canada. Employers in environmental fields could access the database to find employees not only in Canada but in other parts of the world. "Immigrants would thus be able to find work more easily and become certified as Canadian environmental practitioners, while employers could more easily address any skills gaps or labour requirements that they may face" (Stevens 2004).

Bridging Programs

The Ontario government also recognizes the importance of helping immigrants find a niche within the world of work in the province. As Kathleen Wynne, Parliamentary Assistant to the Minister of Training, Colleges and Universities noted: "Ontario's prosperity depends on building an economy based on superior skills and high standards" (McGuinty Government Helping Immigrants Work in Their Chosen Trade or Profession 2004). The Ontario government, in 2004, deployed an investment of $4 million spread over 3 years in projects and services that would facilitate entry into careers for internationally-trained individuals. Among efforts by the Ontario government is the establishment of a bridging program for people with a background and training in pharmacy, teaching and engineering technology.

Another effort to help immigrants with credentials obtain a soft landing in the world of work is the Policy Roundtable Mobilizing Professions and Trades. The experience of one of the members of this board, Fuzail Siddiqui, shows how much waste currently exists in the Canadian system. Siddiqui, who has a master's degree in geology, a doctorate in mineralogy, ten years' teaching experience and 25 years in senior positions in the mining industry could not understand how it could be that he was not receiving any calls after sending résumés for jobs that almost exactly matched his qualifications. Though some individuals such as Carleton University economics professor Christopher Worswick suggests that the education gained abroad may be different or that some of what the immigrants had learned may not be relevant to the Canadian context, Siddiqui responds as follows: "What I smell is fear of the unknown. They don't want to take a chance and it's too much trouble to investigate. If they select me and something goes wrong, they lose their job" (Vu Canada Invites Foreign Workers but Neglects Them on Arrival 2004). This might have struck a chord with some of the government leaders who have taken an interest in helping educated immigrants obtain jobs in their fields. Programs like Career Bridge, which places immigrants with Canadian companies for four months are also a step in the right direction. If fear is indeed the problem why not eliminate this factor by assuring employers that the degrees and credentials brought from abroad are *kosher*. By allowing immigrants to work in a bridging program employers can be assured that the immigrants' abilities indeed match up to what one can expect of similar graduates in Canada. From the bridging programs these immigrant participants can obtain references that can help them move on to more permanent positions elsewhere.

While some professional bodies are in protection mode, safeguarding the jobs of their members from immigrants, others have realized that it is in their own best interest to ensure that immigrants are able to obtain the necessary training in order to participate in the workplace. An example of this is the Ontario Society of Professional Engineers' one year training program. This program answers a legitimate fear that employers have, that the foreign experience might not translate well in a Canadian context. Such practical programs are beneficial because they also help dispel what may be unfounded charges that racism is *always* the reason for not taking immigrants on. Also, the Canadian Council of Professional Engineers (CCPE) has a program of evaluating incoming engineers' credentials, and is just another of the numerous programs currently emerging to ensure that Canada is able to benefit from the expertise of immigrants while also affording immigrants an opportunity to adjust into Canadian society through a job in their field of study or expertise.

From Rocket Scientist to Cinnamon Bun Maker

Most people agree that brain surgeons are smart people. Their job does not leave much room for error. Rocket scientists are perceived to be right up there with brain surgeons, but not when a rocket scientist from China comes to Canada. Ms. Ivy Zheng was so involved in China's program that sent a man into space in 2003 that she won a citation for designing one of the components in the space craft (Immen 2004). One would imagine that the numerous high tech companies in Canada, some of which are involved in aerospace programs would be falling over themselves to hire her. Over the course of two years in Toronto Ms. Zheng could not obtain an engineering job and had to take "a job making cinnamon buns in a shop" (Immen 2004). Ms. Zheng was relentless in her search for a job but could not get anyone in Canada to take her seriously. She also noted that there were many people in her circle with impressive academic and career backgrounds from abroad who were marking time in Canada. Fortunately, Ms. Zheng won a place in the Career Bridge program to serve as an intern with Motorola. This program is supported by the Ontario government and is one of a new crop of programs emerging to help immigrants find work in their pre-immigration careers.

Canadian Virtual University

Another nifty service that has been introduced to assist immigrants is an online resource that aims to help immigrants or potential immigrants finish a Canadian university education quickly. With continual demand on the part of employers for

Canadian education, how would it be if you could produce a Canadian certificate, diploma, or degree when asked? "The resource, which was developed with the funding support of Human Resources Skills Development Canada, is aimed at anyone with foreign education, but especially potential immigrants because it would equip them with a Canadian university degree before arriving in Canada" (Virtual U Helps Immigrants Earn Degrees Before Coming to Canada 2004).

Emancipate Yourself

After receiving numerous racist shocks in Canada you may have learned to "know your place." Thus, instead of trying you have come to believe that you know what the results will be – there is no need to try. One visible minority immigrant who was pursuing a course in gemology, after experiencing various overt and covert acts of racism, gave up on the course, reasoning that it was unlikely any Canadian would give him a job in a jewellery shop. Imagine always being followed every time you enter a convenience shop, a supermarket, department store, or a jewellery shop. Now, who would allow you to be in control of such "precious" merchandise as diamonds and gold necklaces? Several years later, he saw other visible minorities working in jewellery shops and wondered if he had not sabotaged himself by giving up on that dream. With all the negative experiences some immigrants become wary of trying anything; they thus become their own worst enemies. Those who take the plunge often realize that reports of racism may have been exaggerated and that many people in the mainstream do not mind dealing with minorities as customers or clients. It may be true that for the first twenty jobs you applied for you came face to face with racists. But could it be that the 21st person is not a racist? Could it even be that the 21st person is looking for some diversity in her company? Do you not sabotage yourself therefore if you quit too soon? Not a few parents of minority children advise their children to study as hard as they can, believing that in order for visible minorities to get anywhere in Canadian society they have to exhibit superior abilities. If you know that you have the disadvantage of not always being the first choice of potential employers you need to compensate for this handicap (which is no fault of yours) by ensuring that you are, if possible, the best candidate in the pool by far. That way, while some will automatically choose others over you, it is possible that you will encounter many others who will value merit. Wise minority parents may be telling their children to be the Michael Jordans of their professions, the Wayne Gretzkys of their crafts – the real McCoy.

The Heart of a Champion

It is no secret that not all immigrants and refugees coming to Canada speak English or French. For those with minimal language skills the going can be tough.

Government efforts, along with the efforts of community organizations to help these individuals through ESL classes have been very helpful to those who need to improve their language skills. Some in the mainstream, however, point to such expenditure as a waste of taxpayers' resources. So loud has the clamour been that a three-member panel appointed to examine Canada's immigration included a section on the language element. In the 1998 Immigration Legislative Review Advisory Group report *Not Just Numbers: A Canadian Framework for Future Immigration*, the writers noted that being able to speak one of the official languages was important for success. Other studies have also highlighted the importance of speaking one of the official languages. After all, if one cannot communicate one can hardly interact with others, or take advantage of any potential opportunities. As one immigrant from Iran illustrates, however, for those who are motivated to succeed and become contributors to the nation it matters more to be given a chance. When the 37-year-old Siamak Khajepour came to Canada his goal was to obtain a position as a civil engineer, helping to build bridges and buildings as he had done in his home country. Even though in Iran the building codes, which were American and European, did not differ much from the Canadian ones, he still could not get past first base: no Canadian experience, and therefore no career-oriented job. In addition, engineers from outside of Canada needed to work for one year before becoming eligible for a license. The situation seemed hopeless for Mr. Khajepour who left the barren employment landscape of Vancouver at the time for Montreal. Rather than inspecting rivets and struts he found himself "constructing" pizza in a pizzeria. When eventually Mr. Khajepour landed a part-time job with a construction company the language issue was ready to bite him. Did he speak French? No. The uncertainty about hiring him, however, was allayed when Mr. Khajepour offered that he was willing to learn French. He got the job. Four years after he applied for a license Khajepour was issued his engineering license. Like other immigrants eager to contribute he found a job with an engineering firm in Toronto. He may be one of the lucky ones as some have been in Canada for over a decade with no chance of working in their field. Trapped in a factory, a kitchen, or unemployed, their engineering, medical, or other degrees gather dust. Mr. Khajepour, however, is hardly the only immigrant who has come to Canada with less than stellar language abilities and yet achieved remarkable success because of his willingness to learn.

CHAPTER NINE

CANADIAN HIGHER EDUCATIONAL CREDENTIALS AS AN IMPERATIVE

Sheepskin Please

Some immigrants are so eager to work that they take whatever job they can get. The pressure may come from fear of having to depend on welfare or the need to send money to relatives back home as soon as possible. Working long hours, you may come home tired, flop in front of the television, always carrying in your heart desires of improving your prospects through evening courses. But that day never comes. Or you may start a program, but drop out halfway because of difficulty paying the fees. Or the pressure from your relatives back home may be so much that you postpone your educational aspirations indefinitely. One year, two years, five years, ten years. You can't believe you've been in Canada for fifteen years already and you are not doing much better than minimum wage. It must be racism, you think! But buy a copy of the *National Post* or the *Globe and Mail* or any publication in your field of interest and look at the job advertisements. You see letters such as CA (Chartered Accountant); CMA (Certified Management Accountant); CGA (Certified General Accountant); MBA (Master of Business Administration); BA (Bachelor of Arts); M.Sc. (Master of Science); Ph.D. (Doctor of Philosophy). Despite the fact that you finished high school with a good grade, you have never considered yourself one to enter university. Canadians of every background have to demonstrate their qualifications and skills so if you have not established any record of success in the form of credentials your path through the world of work could be tough.

Acquiring knowledge is not enough; Canada is a credential-loving society so you need to have some paper, diploma, to show for your study efforts. Babysitters are being required to take special courses. Kitchen workers are required to take Food Safe courses. Canadian universities offer hundreds of degree, diploma, and certificate courses that help employers to gauge your background and expertise. In some cases, these credentials do nothing more than signal your preparation for more training but all things being equal, someone with credentials will be chosen over someone without. Through education, you are likely to be able to lift yourself and your family out of poverty, and to more confidently engage with your fellow citizens towards the design of a social system that is fair and equitable to all.

B.A., C.A., or BMW?

You have worked hard since you came to Canada. Of course, often you have had to work two jobs just to stay afloat. Over the past ten years you have managed to save enough to buy yourself a BMW. It's a twenty-year-old BMW but a BMW is a BMW is a BMW. Wouldn't it be nice if you could tool around in a brand new one? Earning the right qualifications could bring about a boost in your earnings and make it possible for you to obtain some of the finer things in life. Of course, there may be far more important things in life besides buying a car for you to want to gain higher qualifications. Your greater earning power may make it possible for you to take better care of your family and to meet financial obligations that you could not easily meet in the past.

Get a Leg Up with Canadian Education

Immigrants who enter the Canadian educational system gain an advantage over their counterparts who come with degrees from other countries. This is because one of the persistent problems faced by immigrants is the lack of recognition of their professional qualifications in Canada. Thus, we have well qualified doctors from India languishing in the obscurity of stockrooms across the land; we have engineers from Egypt who are stuck with working in restaurants, and former professors from Asia who may not even be allowed into a kindergarten classroom! An engineer from Hong Kong who had initial difficulties of breaking into the Canadian job market decided to enter the British Columbia Institute of Technology to boost his chances. As this individual noted, "People like me have expertise in our mother countries but can't get experience here. That's where education comes in" (Stevens 2004).

Immigrants who attend university in Canada eliminate one of the barriers that they are often faced with, namely, lack of recognition for their qualifications. Also, many university programs in Canada now come with co-operative options that allow for work opportunities. This means that it is possible to graduate with about a year or 18-months of work experience under your belt. This also makes it difficult for potential employers to say that you do not have Canadian experience. Your dream of potentially buying a brand new BMW is not dead just yet.

Some immigrants obtain additional qualifications in Canada to strengthen their résumé. Eugene Yeung, who came to Canada from Hong Kong, found himself unable to obtain a job as an engineer after going through a costly immigration process. Rather than give up he decided to enroll in the one-year Bachelor of Environmental Technology program at BCIT, an institution that has a good reputation for the success of its graduates (Stevens 2004). Another immigrant, Sunny Mangat, who had a Master's degree in environmental technology from India and an Information Technology Systems certificate from the United Kingdom decided to obtain a

Master's in engineering from the University of Manitoba as a complement.

Educational Options

By all measures, Canada has one of the best educational systems in the world. For some immigrants, therefore, the chance to benefit from the educational system is a great incentive for coming to Canada. In some parts of the world such as Hong Kong and Taiwan, education at the elementary and high school levels is very competitive and some parents believe that the system is not flexible enough. To get their children to become more flexible in their thinking they seek the benefit of a North American education for their children. Some also cite the relative ease of entering university in Canada compared to their home country. This may be true but going through university in Canada can be a real challenge for those who are not adequately prepared. The second part of this book addresses strategies that can help make your educational career a breeze. Some foreign students who considered themselves quite brilliant in their home countries have struggled within the Canadian university system and not a few have had to fight tooth and nail to maintain their grades and to avoid being kicked out. Making use of the strategies in Part II will help you get more out of your university experience.

The Dog Ate My Transcript, Honest

Refugees, in particular, who may want to continue their education might face some initial challenges. Individuals who had to leave their home country under pressure may not have access to their educational transcripts, which might facilitate their re-entry into the school system in Canada. In North America it is taken for granted that if one wants one's school transcripts all one has to do is contact the institution in question. Thus, Canadian school administrators might often not understand those cases when immigrants make the claim that even though they have completed high school or university they cannot get hold of their transcripts. This may seem laughable but it is a reality that many people from Third World countries are familiar with. Immigrants and refugees may have to press their folks back in the mother country to help secure any evidence of their prior schooling or else be willing to take challenge examinations that can facilitate their entry into school in Canada. The point is that when faced with such barriers it is easy to give up or to postpone indefinitely one's plan to go to school. It is frustrating when, for example, the immigrant offers to take some form of qualifying exam and is told that would not do, and that only the transcript would do. Some immigrants give up in frustration, chalking it up to just one more attempt by people in the mainstream to frustrate their advancement.

There are established procedures in Canada to which you need to be aware. Some of these may seem unfair but rather than give up why not redouble your efforts to seek other equally acceptable ways that will help you gain admission. Sometimes all you have to do is ask and the right way will be pointed out to you.

Know When to be Humble

If indeed, you completed high school but have no proof, instead of giving up on continuing your education, why not consider some of the bridging programs offered by community colleges. These usually start with an assessment test from where you can progress beyond language courses to specific subject areas of interest to you. Don't worry that the language course seems "beneath" what you perceive to be your true ability. It will become obvious pretty soon into the course if that is the case. But what if you start an upgrading course and you discover that the material is challenging and that you are even struggling to keep up. Then quite possibly, you needed the course and that it is in your own best interest to apply yourself to it. Being "forced" to repeat a grade for which you feel qualified might appear like a waste of time. But compare that to the folly of not having the chance to further your education because of a little too much pride.

Let Your Confidence Show

In many countries around the world, including those in Asia and Africa, humility is highly prized. This means that people who may be accomplished in one field or another may find it awkward to "praise" themselves when asked about their accomplishments. They may be aware that they are really good at what they do and yet when asked they might self-effacingly dismiss their achievements as being nothing at all. This attitude, however, does not wash in Canada. In Canada, if you are capable of doing something you had better say so with all the confidence you can muster and be prepared to back that up. If you say that you are not all that good a job interviewer might take you at your word and decide that someone with more expertise should be given the opportunity.

Don't let the everyday frustrations get you down. Remember what it took you to get where you are. Let your confidence shine through.

Mentors

If Canadians came to live in your home country while you were there you would no doubt have felt that they could not instantly have a full understanding of the norms of the society. This may very well be true and being a native son or daughter you would probably have been eager to show the "foreigners" the dos and don'ts in the society. It is no different now that you are the "foreigner." Whether in regards to the workplace or matters of everyday life there is much that you can glean from the newspapers, television and other news sources. For maximum results, however, it is a good idea to find someone who will be your mentor or coach. Government programs and personal efforts have managed to get some minorities into jobs but often these people have not been able to advance because of lack of effective mentoring for them.

Distance Learning or On-Campus

For those who are working and feel the need to continue doing so, one option for upgrading or acquiring Canadian qualifications may be through distance learning, a growing field in Canada. In the resources section (Chapter 10/page 86) you can find information about Canadian distance learning programs. The list is by no means exhaustive but it can give you an idea of some of the possibilities. Your own enquiries and research could yield much, much more in the way of educational options in Canada.

Canadian Virtual University, mentioned earlier, is actually a consortium of leading Canadian universities that offer distance and online degrees. There are over 250 Canadian degrees, certificates and diplomas available through the consortium. Foreign credentials can be evaluated through a group affiliated with the consortium and if there is a gap that needs to be filled, the individual can take the necessary courses. As Vicky Busch, Executive Director of CVU notes: "It's not that immigrants aren't educated... A 2001 Statistics Canada survey showed that 72% of immigrants have post-secondary education. Rather, it's that employers aren't sure what a degree or diploma from an unknown school in a foreign country means. We offer immigrants a speedier route to a recognized Canadian credential that employers more readily understand" (Virtual U Helps Earn Degrees Before Coming to Canada 2004).

Get Involved

The challenges that we face in the world today are enormous. The lack of education at a basic level is one problem that many governments are doing their best to solve, though the solutions are not coming fast enough. Even in the so-called advanced countries such as Canada it is shocking to read about the large number of functional illiterates. If you want to be a contributor to Canadian society and perhaps to the world you will, like others who leveraged their education to bring change to the world, take your education seriously and aim to be a lifelong learner. Canada may not be a perfect place but it is a land that has opened its heart to people from all over the world and is hoping that this experiment in having the world together in this blessed land will pay dividends in promoting peace rather than sowing hatred. The last two Governors General, Adrienne Clarkson and Michaëlle Jean, are immigrants from

minority racial and cultural groups. Won't you reach out to your fellow Canadians --
and for the stars!!!

CHAPTER TEN

'SMART' GOAL SETTING AND WHY

Goal setting is powerful. It helps you clarify what may be a jumble of wishes, desires, and wants in your mind into something concrete. Writing your goals down can add an element of commitment to your efforts to achieve what may have been nebulous in your mind. It's important to have short, medium, and long-term goals. Extreme rigidity, however, has no place in smart goal setting. Imagine your goal is to walk to the nearest convenience shop from your home. You determine that taking Printemps Road will be the most direct route. When you get on Printemps Road you realize that work crews have dug their way clear across the road. The pavement is blocked and there are large signs saying, "Road closed. Men (and women) at work. Road will re-open in 3 months." Clearly you are not going to wait for Printemps Road to re-open before you get yourself that cup of noodle soup that you crave. Too bad Printemps Road is closed but you make your way back and take a slightly longer route. Actually it only adds five minutes to your little trip. That sure beats three months' wait. Moreover, now you know not to take Printemps Road until three months have passed. The same goes with goal setting. Know what you want and be flexible in how to achieve that end. Experts on goal setting have come up with a proven goal setting reminder, SMART, which you can use to guide you.

S = **Specific**
M = **Measurable**
A = **Achievable**
R = **Realistic**
T = **Time-Bound**

Specific – Your goals should be specific. Being specific has much more power to move your mind compared to carrying hazy notions around. I want to earn an MBA in Information Technology is much more specific than I want to earn an MBA. With a more specific goal, you are better able to direct your efforts.

Measurable – Your goal should be measurable. Olympic athletes and indeed sports people go into competition knowing exactly what the demands of the event might be. They are timed; their efforts are measured. This allows for better scorekeeping. Having two master's degrees or speaking five languages are measurable in the same way that you can measure your proficiency in piano playing by taking the Royal Conservatory of Music level exams.

Achievable – You have an idea of what you are capable of. Be sure that what you want to do can indeed be done. Granted, there are times when others might believe that your goal is unachievable. However be sure that in your own mind it is something that can be achieved. Before Roger Bannister ran the mile in four minutes it was considered impossible by many experts. Since he broke that record many more people have followed suit. Remember though that trying to do the improbable carries a risk. Not a few people perished trying to conquer Mt. Everest before Sir Edmund Hillary and Sherpa Tenzing Norgay succeeded in doing it. Since then, more people have perished trying to climb the highest mountain in the world. Is your goal to stand on Mt. Logan and scratch the moon? Watch out.

Realistic – Being realistic means being aware of the resources you have available or what you are able to lay your hands on. There are times when you have to enlist the support of others to achieve a particular goal. The pyramids, the Taj Mahal, the Panama Canal, and assorted other wonders of the world may seem unrealistic in execution to the average person, but for those who have the expertise and the technical knowledge these were wholly realistic and realizable goals.

Time-bound – Giving yourself a deadline to accomplish something helps you put more energy into whatever the project might be. Without a deadline there is no pressure or incentive to get moving.

List your most important goals:

1. _____

2. _____

3. _____

4. _____

5. _____

Why

   SMART goals, powerful as they are, pack more punch when they are invested with a bit of emotion. It is thus important to consider **why** you want to achieve a particular goal.

No.	Specific goal	Why	'Achieve by' date	How to achieve
E.g.	Buy a 3-bedroom condo in Saanich	More comfort for my family	Jan. 20XX	From this month, will save an extra $300/mo towards down payment
1				
2				
3				
4				
5				

Revisit your goals from time to time. Check on how you're coming along. Congratulate yourself for goals achieved and then set new goals. One young man had been working in a high-end retail shop for three years. He was a manager in charge of the displays both on the floor and in the window. One holiday season he returned home to visit his parents and while in his old room he came across one of his notebooks from high school. In it he had written: *I will be an architect.* All the reasons why he had wanted to be an architect came flooding back to him. He had been inspired to become an architect while on a vacation in Italy but as he struggled to make ends meet in the city these old dreams had withered. When he returned to the city he started making enquiries in the schools of design and architecture. He found a program he liked and submitted his application, which was accepted. He gave his notice, quit the job and entered architecture school. He had always had a nagging feeling that something was missing in his life even though to the younger employees in the retail shop he was quite a success. Entering architecture school was his big dream. Some of your dreams might have fallen by the wayside as you've laboured through the workaday world. Some of your dreams have been covered by so much dust you will need to do some real dusting for days before you get to them. Remember, at the end of the day, you can't blame the system for letting you down. You can't sit the "system" down and say, "Look at what you've done to my life." It is up to you to navigate your way through the system. As difficult as things might be, you will find that there is always someone who is thriving in spite of it. What makes the difference? Why have some given up, while others continue to strive and see success for their efforts? Be on the side of those who never give up. Why not be on the side of those who say that no matter how difficult things might be, "I'll see my dreams through." Live up to your God-given potential. Won't you?

REMINDERS AND RESOURCES

These resources are by no means exhaustive but give you an idea of the range of services available. Check with community associations in your local area for information on specific services and for referrals.

Information is King

You may already be familiar with the global reach of the Internet. And you may have used the library frequently in your home country. Now is not the time to stop. In Canada, you can gain access to most public libraries without having to pay. To borrow books, however, you may have to prove that you live in the city where the library is located; the library will give you specific details about what is required. Many libraries across Canada offer free Internet service. Other possible sources, of course, include making use of Internet service cafes, a listing of which might be found in your telephone book, or simply by having your own computer access at home or through a wireless laptop.

ACCENT REDUCTION

Look in your local yellow pages under language instruction and inquire about specific programs geared towards accent reduction in your local area. You may be able to buy tapes or CDs on accent reduction in any of the major bookstores.

Web site: http://www.americanaccent.com

CREDIT

Credit is very important in Canada. In fact, having a regular credit card or a Department store credit card may be very useful in helping you establish credit – in other words your credibility in the society. If you prove that you are a good credit risk there may be many opportunities for you to gain access to funds when you need it. Unfortunately if you mismanage such credit, however, you may end up having a bad credit rating. Therefore if you must use credit, please be careful. Bad credit will get reported to credit reporting agencies and remain on your file for seven years.

Credit Reporting Agencies

Equifax Canada
Consumer Relations Department
Box 190 Jean Talon Station
Montreal, Quebec
H1S 2Z2
Tel: 514-493-2314 or Toll free: 1-800-465-7166
to request a copy of your report

TransUnion
Consumer Relations Centre
P.O. Box 338, LCD 1
Hamilton, Ontario
L8L 7W2

For Quebec Residents:
TransUnion (Echo Group)
1600 boul. Henri Bourassa Ouest, Suite 210
Montreal, Quebec
H3M 3E2

Employment Insurance (EI)

Unemployed Canadians can receive temporary assistance through this government program. While on EI the applicant needs to be looking for a job or retraining for another occupation. Employment Insurance may also be available for Canadians who are sick, pregnant or caring for a newborn or adopted child. In addition those who must care for a family member with a serious illness, particularly one with high possibility of death, may qualify.

Federal Government Services

Calling the toll free number, 1-800-622-6232 can put you in touch with federal government programs and services.

Identity Papers

In Canada, there are some documents that are so important that you should always know exactly where yours are at any given time. These include your Driver's Licence, Social Insurance card, Health Insurance card, and your Record of Landing

(IMM 1000). You may find it useful to carry these documents as you visit government agencies, banks, and in practically any sphere of activity where your identity needs to be established. Citizenship and Immigration Canada advises, however, that the originals of the permanent resident papers should be kept safely at home or in a safe deposit box, while a photocopy is carried around.

Warning

Under no circumstance should you lend your social insurance or health card to others; this could lead to a loss of the relevant benefits as well as potential identity theft.

Telephone Directories

The major telephone companies in your area can provide you a copy of the telephone directory. In smaller cities the white pages (residential) and yellow pages (business) come in one book; in the bigger cities there may be separate white and yellow pages directories. The blue pages within the white pages list government services.

Telephone Providers

When you subscribe for telephone service, you will get detailed information about the payment options. Usually, there is a wide range of services, such as call forwarding, blocking of your long distance service if you are afraid of running huge bills, etc. Do consider if you really need all the options because often the extras come at a price, which can add up pretty quickly. Read very carefully any brochures or information packets provided by the telephone company, or for that matter, any agency. This is because once you sign your name to an agreement it is a contract that is enforceable, so be diligent in appraising any services you sign up for. This can save you much heartache in the future.

Bell Canada (Eastern Canada)
Toll free: 1-800-668-6878

Telus (Western Canada)
Toll free: 1-888-811-2323

Alternative Telephone Provider (prepaid services)
Canada Reconnect
885 Dunsmuir Street
Vancouver, BC
V6C 1N5
Toll free: 1-800-930-6644

Transition Services

Immigrant-serving agencies help newcomers with issues relating to settlement. The range of services may include the following, which may be tackled directly or through referral to another agency:

- Finding housing
- Upgrading language skills
- Finding a job
- Dealing with spousal abuse
- Providing family support
- Providing day care services

COMMUNITY SUPPORT

Council on African Canadian Education
Trade Mart Building, 5th Floor
2021 Brunswick Street
P.O. Box 578
Halifax, Nova Scotia
B3J 2S9
Tel: 902-424-2678
Fax: 902-424-7210
Email: CACE@gov.ns.ca

- Focuses on the development of Africentric educational philosophy, approaches, and interventions. Also curriculum development, research, teacher education, publishing, and community educational development.
- Assists students to improve their understanding and grades in school. They have been in operation since 1979.

City of Toronto: Information for New Immigrants
Web site: http://www.city.toronto.on.ca/immigration/employment.htm

Government of Ontario
Gateway to Diversity
Web site: http://www.equalopportunity.on.ca/eng_g/index.asp

ISAP (Immigrant Settlement and Adaptation Program)
Web site: http://www.kwymca.org/Contribute/immigrant/program_ISAP.asp

A.R. Kaufman Family YMCA
333 Carwood Avenue
Kitchener, Ontario
N2G 3C5
Tel: 519-743-5201
* Other centres available

Jamaican Canadian Association
995 Arrow Road
Toronto, Ontario
M9M 2Z5
Tel: 416-746-5772
Fax: 416-746-7035
Email: info@jcassoc.org
Website: http://www.jcassoc.com

- Assists African Canadians and works to promote Black/Jamaican culture.

LINC (Language Instruction for Newcomers)
Web site: http://www.tbs-sct.gc.ca/rma/common/us-nous_e.asp

- LINC program provides support for adult newcomers who want to improve their English
- LINC facilitates the social, cultural and economic integration of immigrants and refugees into Canada.

Ottawa Community Immigrant Services Organization
959 Wellington Street
Ottawa, Ontario
K1Y 4W1
Web site: http://www.ociso.org/

PEI Association for Newcomers to Canada
179 Queen Street
Box 2846
Charlottetown, PEI
C1A 8C4
Tel: 902-628-6009
Fax: 902-894-4928
Web site: http://www.peianc.com

S.U.C.C.E.S.S.
Greater Vancouver, British Columbia
Web site: http://www.success.bc.ca/eng/

- Serves about 78,000 clients annually
- 11 offices in the Lower Mainland area
- Has approximately 4,000 volunteers
- Offers services in English, Mandarin, Cantonese, and other languages
- Has an office at the airport to help immigrants as soon as they disembark
- Gets immigrants into the community
- Programs include: job training, immigration settlement, English as a Second Language training, etc.

CREDENTIAL EVALUATION SERVICES

Academic Credentials Evaluation Service (ACES)
York University, Office of Admissions
Student Services Centre
4700 Keele Street
Toronto, Ontario
M3J 1P3
Tel: 416-736-5787
Web site: http://www.yorku.ca/admissio/aces.asp

Comparative Evaluation for Studies Done Outside Quebec
Web site: http://www.immigration-quebec.gouv.qc.ca/anglais/education/

International Credential Assessment Service of Canada
147 Wyndham Street North, Suite 409
Guelph, Ontario
N1H 4E9
Tel: 519-763-7282 or Toll free in Canada: 1-800-321-6021
Fax 519-763-6964
Web site: http://www.icascanada.ca/English/main.html

International Credential Evaluation Service
4355 Mathissi Place
Burnaby, British Columbia
V5G 4S8
Tel: 604-431-3402
Toll free in British Columbia: 1-800-663-1663 (local #3402)
Fax: 604-431-3382
Web site: http://www.ola.bc.ca/ices/

International Qualifications Assessment Service (IQAS)
Ministry of Learning, Government of Alberta
4th Floor, Sterling Place, 9940-106 Street
Edmonton, Alberta
T5K 2N2
Tel: 780-427-2655
Fax: 780-422-9734

The Manitoba Academic Credential Report
Manitoba Labour and Immigration
Settlement and Labour Market Services Branch
5th Floor, 213 Notre Dame Avenue
Winnipeg, Manitoba
R3B 1N3
Tel: 204-945-6300
Fax: 204-948-2148
Web site: http://www.immigratemanitoba.com

- Free to Manitoba residents

Stepping Stones to Success,
Recognizing Foreign Credentials and Qualifications
in Prince Edward Island
Web site: www.peianc.com/docs/qr_report.pdf

University of Toronto Comparative Education Service (CES)
Web site: http://www.adm.utoronto.ca/ces/

World Education Services
45 Charles Street East, Suite 700
Toronto, Ontario
M4Y 1S2
Tel: 416-972-0070 or toll free: 1-866-343-0070
Fax: 416-972-9004
Web site: http://www.wes.org/ca/index.asp

DISTANCE LEARNING

Canada Online Education
Web site: http://www.online-education.net/canada_schools.html

Accredited online degree information worldwide
Web site: http://www.degree.net

- This site, run by Dr. John Bear, one of the foremost authorities on distance learning, has lists of accredited distance learning programs around the world including Bachelor's, Master's and Doctorates.

Canadian Virtual University
Web site: http://www.cvu-uvc.ca/

- Consortium of leading Canadian universities offering distance education. Over 250 degree courses through the Internet or by distance education

HEARING IMPAIRED

The Canadian Hearing Society
Toronto Regional Office
271 Spadina Road
Toronto, Ontario M5R 2V3
Tel: 416-928-2504 Voice
Tel: 416-964-0023 TTY
Fax: 416-928-2523

HIGHER EDUCATION

Community and Technical Colleges
Web site: http://cset.sp.utoledo.edu/canctcol.html

- Provides links to Canadian technical, community, and business colleges

Community Colleges
Association of Canadian Community Colleges
Web site: http://www.accc.ca/english/index.cfm
* Member institutions and website links available at the above web address

Universities
The Association of Universities and Colleges of Canada represents 92 Canadian public and private non-profit universities and university-degree level colleges.
Web site: http://www.aucc.ca/about_us/membership/ourmemb_e.html
* List of universities and colleges available on the above website

IMMIGRATION

Citizenship and Immigration Canada
Web site: http://www.cic.gc.ca

Gain access to application kits and guides; recent announcements; reports, publications, and other information that can facilitate living for you in Canada.

Toll free from anywhere in Canada: 1-888-242-2100
Montreal area – Tel: 514-496-1010
Toronto area – Tel: 416-973-4444
Vancouver area – Tel: 604-666-2171

Welcome to Canada: What You Should Know
Web site: http://www.cic.gc.ca/english/newcomer/wel-10.e.html

JOB RELATED ASSISTANCE

Bilingualxpress
Web site: http://www.bilingualxpress.ca/

- Bilingual jobs Toronto

Career Gateway
Web site: http://edu.gov.on.ca/eng/career/

- Ontario Ministry of Education

Centre Génération Emploi Inc.
414-7000 Av. du Parc
Montreal, Quebec
H3N 1X1
Tel: 514-948-0000
Fax: 514-948-5097

- Employment training service

City of Toronto, Human resources
Web site: http://www.city.toronto.on.ca/employment/

- How to look for work in Canada
- Employment with the City of Toronto
- Employment with the Government of Canada
- Employment with the Province of Ontario
- Job sites
- Self-employment
- Education credentials
- Community resources
- How to prepare a résumé
- Social insurance number (SIN)
- Training

Contact Point
Web site: http://www.contactpoint.ca/

- **Career resources, learning, and networking**

Electronic Labour Exchange
Web site: http://www.jobsetc.ca

Employment Insurance (EI)
Web site: http://www.hrsdc.gc.ca/en/gateways/nav/top_nav/program/ei.shtml

Gateway to Diversity.
Web site: http://www.equalopportunity.on.ca/eng_g/apt/index.asp

Human Resources Development Canada (HRDC)
Web site: http://www.hrdc-drhc.gc.ca/

Has a number of programs and services to help Canadians seeking employment or participation in their communities. Also maintains a job bank.

Jobs Canada
Web site: http://jobcanada.org/

Job Futures – Government of Canada
Web site: http://jobfutures.ca/en/home.shtml

Nevian Consulting & Placement Services Inc.
The Madison Centre
4950 Yonge Street, Suite 2200
Toronto, Ontario
M2N 6K1
Tel: 416-805-9636
Email: info@ncps.ca
Web site: http://www.ncps.ca/contact.htm

- Bilingual Recruitment Specialists

Prospects: Ontario's Guide to Career Planning
Web site: http://www.edu.gov.on.ca/eng/general/elemsec/job/prospect/index.html

Workopolis
Web site: http://www.workopolis.com

One of the largest gateways for jobs in Canada; includes links for education and skills upgrading as well as advice for job seekers and the employed alike.

Vitesse Reskilling
1200 Montreal Road, Building M-50
Ottawa, ON K1A 0R6
Canada
Tel.: 613-746-3595
Fax: 613-746-6653
Email: info@vitesse.ca
Web site: www.vitesse.ca/

Provides retraining for graduates in the science and engineering field to enable them to take advantage of current and emerging opportunities in software engineering, photonics, bioinformatics, microelectronics, wireless communications, and related fields.

WorldSkills: Competition for Excellence in the Skilled Trades
Jeff Wilson, Bid Manager
2009 WorldSkills Calgary Bid Organizing Committee
Tel: 403-210-5744
Fax: 403-284-8940
Email: jeff.wilson@sait.ca

Volunteer Opportunities Exchange
Web site: http://www.voe-reb.org/

PUBLIC SPEAKING

Toastmasters International
Web site: http://www.toastmasters.org

- Public speaking organization. Clubs all across Canada and indeed worldwide. For those who must lead.

SELF-EMPLOYMENT SUCCESS

Business Development Centre
#501-1788 West Broadway
Vancouver, B.C.
V6J 1Y1
Contact: Thomas Tam, Program Director
Tel: 604-732-3278
Fax: 604-732-9818
Email: fctam@success.bc.ca

- Services: Confidential business counselling
- Referral Services: Referral to professional agencies, government agencies, and community services
- Resource Services: Business resources and information, literature and material translation, business events calendar, brochures
- Training Courses
- Self-Employment Program
- Entrepreneurial Training for Business Immigrants
- Business and Language Training for Youth
- Small Business Management Training
- Importing and Exporting Business Training
- Business Communication Training
- Business Computer Software Training
- Training Seminars
- Business Start-Up
- Taxation

- Financial Strategies
- Marketing
- Franchising
- Licensing
- Commercial Leasing
- Labour Standards
- Networking
- Community and Business Organizations
- Government Agencies
- Professional Organizations
- Arrangement of Business Visits and Tours
- Business Conferences and Trade Fairs

TUTORIAL SERVICES

Higher Marks Educational Institute
1440 Bathurst St.
Toronto, Ontario
M5R 3J3

PART II

CONNECTING TO CANADIAN ACADEMIA FROM THE MARGINS OF SOCIETY

Higher Education is a meta-strategic resource in Canadian society, and the greater majority of racial and cultural minorities that have experienced success in Canadian society from the margins acquired and utilized the appropriate qualifications or credentials from mainstream Canadian academia. It requires strategic resources such as relevant knowledge about how Canadian academia operates and cutting-edge academic skills to negotiate the minefields of the Canadian school system in order to facilitate one's success. Therefore, new immigrants, refugees and international students who enter Canadian academia need these strategic resources.

An international student was shocked when she first started a Master's program in Canada after graduating with an Honours Bachelor's Degree from an English-speaking African country. In her graduate classes and the undergraduate class for which she was a teaching assistant she observed that students could interrupt the professor with questions and comments. The amount of reading per week was overwhelming to her. She was also surprised that class participation was graded and doing oral presentations and writing term papers were the main assessment criteria for the courses she was taking. It was very devastating to her when her first term paper did not pass, and the professor stated in his comments that this graduate student had a writing problem and should see the Writing Centre for help. She was accused, among other things, of lack of clarity, lack of critical/analytical thinking, and making use of other people's ideas without properly acknowledging them. Moreover, the grades for her first semester examinations were shockingly low. These comments and grades were more devastating because this student graduated in her home university at the top of her class. Sounds familiar? Many international students, new immigrants and refugees experience some level of this academic culture shock when they begin their academic programs in Canadian educational institutions.

To succeed in Canadian academia, international students, new immigrants and refugees need to overcome this initial culture shock. Whatever their field of study—natural/physical sciences, social sciences, humanities, business---they need to effectively connect to the Canadian academic culture from the margins. This academic culture projects the ideals of critical or analytical thinking, logical reasoning, effective communication, problem identification, problem solving, etc. In order to meet these academic cultural goals international students, new immigrants and refugees in the mainstream school system need to acquire and apply the high level skills of focused listening, critical thinking and reading, academic writing, class participation, academic note taking/making, strategies for taking examinations, and academic research and presentation. Regular courses in Canadian post-secondary institutions do not directly teach these skills. It is assumed that the student already has these skills presumably from the High School system, and if they do not have the skills they should acquire them on their own. Writing/Learning Centres in Canadian post-secondary educational institutions are established for this particular purpose.

This part of the book tries to fill this gaping hole for international students, new immigrants and refugees in the school system who lack these strategic resources to do well in Canadian academia. Providing these minorities in the education system with the fundamental knowledge and skills highlighted in the chapters of this section of the book is essential. This is because inequalities, racism and ethnocentrism in Canadian society compel these minorities to connect to the education system from the margins of society where these strategic resources are generally lacking.

CHAPTER ELEVEN

EDUCATION IN CANADA:
MINORITIES CONNECTING TO MAINSTREAM
CURRICULUM AND INSTRUCTION FROM THE MARGINS

Introduction

As in many countries in the global community, there is increasing emphasis on formal education in Canada with the assumption that such education produces a productive labor force and useful citizens. With this assumption Canada provides expanded educational opportunities at all levels for its citizens. Federal and Provincial governments, First Nations communities, and private institutions fund and operate elementary, secondary, post-secondary education and vocational training programs. There is diversity of educational delivery methods: classroom-based, internet-based, distance, and a combination of them. Classroom-based education is the most predominant in Canada, but on-line delivery modes are growing very quickly. Elementary, Middle and High Schools in Canada are virtually tuition free. However tuition and books are not free at the post-secondary level. The post-secondary and vocational systems are subsidized by the government but students have to pay fees to cover the difference between government subsidy and the operating costs of educational institutions. Many scholarships are available to post-secondary students who have outstanding grades, excel in sports and/or contribute substantially to community development. Needy students can access various bursaries. Students from low-income families and other low-income students qualify for student loans to help them fund their education. Due to increasing tuition fees and the high cost of educational materials, many Canadian students work at least part-time to help pay their way through school. The above characteristics of Canadian education generally present opportunities and challenges to new immigrants, refugees and international students.

Opportunities and Inequalities

Given the expanded educational opportunities in Canada it is not surprising that statistically Canada is counted among the developed nations with the highest number of their citizens holding post-secondary educational qualifications, particularly university degrees (Wotherspoon 2004).

The formal educational opportunities have expanded more for Canadian women than any other group. Since 1981 females have represented the greater majority of students in the formal education system, and they outperform males at all levels with the exception of PhD level (Davies and Guppy 1998). Likewise, the educational expansion has also benefited some racial and ethnic minorities in Canada who were historically excluded. According to Davies and Guppy (1998), "the educational differences between racial and ethnic groups appear to have disappeared or diminished significantly in recent decades." It is important to remark, however, that Aboriginal people, Francophones within Quebec, Canadian-born Blacks, and Portuguese Canadians are still under-represented as compared to other groups (Wotherspoon 2004). This suggests that despite the expanded educational opportunities it is not all Canadians that equally benefit from the formal education system. The mainstream teacher-student relations, curriculum objective and materials, standards for assessing and evaluating students and the general social climate within Canadian educational institutions do not work for these students because of their cultural and socio-economic backgrounds as well as racial/ethnic discrimination (Dei 1994 and 1996, Kelly 1998, Adu-Febiri 2003/04, Wotherspoon 2004).

The incessant critiques and protests from minority and women professors, race/ethnic relations and feminist scholars and activists from the grassroots have resulted in increasing sensitivity to, but not elimination of, the impacts of gender, social class, and racial/ethnic discrimination in the Canadian school system. As Dei (1996) clearly puts it, Euro-Canadian hegemony continues to function and organize the structures within which the delivery of education operates. And Kelly (1998) argues that this hegemony goes beyond race/ethnicity. In her words, "Generally [Canadian] schools produce many different raced, classed and gendered identities as they rank and sort students using the curriculum" (Kelly 1998, p. 123). In light of the above research it could be concluded that the female, lower class and racial/ethnic minority students who succeed in the education system do so mainly because they connect from the margins to the mainstream educational requirements, standards and expectations, and hardly because the Canadian education system is non-racist, non-sexist and non-classist. Therefore, until gender, social class and racial/ethnic sensitivities and equity saturate the education system, new immigrants, refugees, international students and other minorities have to likewise connect from the margins to the mainstream educational culture if they are to succeed in Canadian education.

Many new immigrants enter Canada with secondary or post-secondary edu-cational credentials but are compelled to repeat their education in Canada if they hope to be considered for jobs in Canada. Likewise, to be employable refugees need to obtain Canadian formal education credentials. Coming from education systems different from Canada's and due to racism and other barriers, these new immigrants and refugees have to connect to the mainstream Canadian educational curriculum and pedagogy from the margins in order to receive credentials they need to look for work.

Curriculum and Instruction

The curriculum and instruction of the Canadian formal education system operate to construct uniformity among students through conformity to the mainstream academic culture. The core of the education system is Francocentric in Quebec and Anglocentric in the rest of Canada. Diversity is hardly practised in the crucial areas of teacher employment, educational materials, curriculum, instructional styles, and so on (Fleras and Elliott 2002).

Notwithstanding this Eurocentric Canadian education system, the quality of its content and instruction are perceived as very high relative to standards in other countries. Many international students are therefore attracted to the Canadian school system every year. To succeed, these international students, like new immigrants and refugees, have to connect to the standards and expectations of Canadian educational requirements from the margins mainly because of the silencing of substantive diversity in the education system.

Connecting Without Assimilating

The biggest challenge to new immigrants, refugees and international students, like all non-mainstream Canadians, is how to connect to the education requirements and standards that espouse mainstream experiences and values without being absorbed into the mainstream Canadian Anglocentric and Francocentric educational culture. Until multiculturalism and anti-racism education take front and center stage of the Canadian education system, these students have to rely on their family and ethnic community resources to maintain the core of their original cultures while connecting to the education system. They have to develop bifurcated lives. To facilitate this bifurcation, students need to be very conscious of the fact that the school system is assimilative at the core but it is possible to resist assimilation by aiming at obtaining credentials from the system without absorbing its values and beliefs. Although difficult to manage a bifurcated life between school and out-of-school cultures, many Asian-, African-, Arab- and Hispanic-Canadians have succeeded in doing this with the help of home and community support.

Conclusion

In effect, in this era that multiculturalism and anti-racism education are peripheral to the Canadian education system, immigrants, refugees, international students and other minorities have to connect to the schooling system without being absorbed by the educational culture. They can achieve high grades in school without assimilating. This could be done by mastering the fundamental knowledge and skills to score high grades for credentials while systematically keeping the creeping core of mainstream culture at bay. The following chapters discuss these basic knowledge and skills, and suggest strategies students can use to master them so as to enhance their chances of succeeding in the school system from the margins.

CHAPTER TWELVE

ACQUIRING CRITICAL THINKING SKILLS TO SUCCEED IN THE CANADIAN ACADEMIC CULTURE

This chapter is essentially a reprint of an article written by Francis Adu-Febiri and first published as "Thinking Skills in Education: Ideal and Real Academic Cultures" in the CDTL Brief, a publication of the Centre for Development of Teaching and Learning, National University of Singapore, Vol. 5 No. 4, pp.1-3.

Introduction

Thinking, that is, the ability to reason systematically with logic and evidence is a valuable human attribute. One family I know, realizing the importance of thinking skills in life, made it their focused objective to raise their children to be "thinkers rather than reflectors of other peoples' ideas." What this family seems to know is that thinking is learned and can help their children become original, creative, and innovative problem-solvers. This knowledge seems to be illusive to society and the education system in many countries, particularly developing countries. Hence, unlike this family, many educational systems in the global village do not systematically develop thinking skills in students. Similarly, the cultures of many societies do not develop a normative system to support thinking. In my own education up to the bachelor's level, nobody consciously or systematically showed/taught me how to think. No wonder I was so frustrated the first year of my graduate program that required me to do systematic thinking. Because of the usefulness of thinking skills and my frustrating experience in my schooling, I have made it a personal policy in my teaching to introduce thinking skills to my students through my course organization and delivery.

Despite the prevalence of such surface learning approach to learning in many educational institutions, one of the major expectations of the physical sciences, social sciences and humanities is that they produce students skilled in critical thinking. According to Giarrusso *et al* (2001, p. 8), college students are expected to understand entire systems of knowledge, and to develop analytical reasoning and thinking. At the upper level the culture of academia rewards the analytical mind, and an analytical mind is developed through critical thinking. Therefore, in order to excel in the upper levels of academia you have to practice critical thinking in verbal class participation, reading, researching, writing, and oral presentation.

What Critical Thinking Is

As O'Day (1991, p. 31) insightfully observes, critical thinking is about:

➤ Assessing the credibility of what you hear, read, and present. Don't take anything for granted; don't accept anything at face value. Question everything.
➤ Understanding what you read/hear/say, and then questioning it:
  • Stating something as fact: is there a reasonable basis for such a statement?
  • Offering an opinion: is it reasonable or is there some basis for refuting it?
  • Conclusions: based on feelings, circumstantial evidence or fact?
  • Ideas: are particular ideas pushed to the exclusion of others?
  • Motives: are there ulterior motives underlying the statement?

In effect, critical thinking is the process of revealing the extent to which the reasons and evidence given to support an idea or argument are TRUE or FACTUAL, and if the idea or argument meets the requirement of LOGIC.

• TRUTH: A matter of fact.
• LOGIC: Systematic and consistent reasoning.
• Example: Is the following statement true? Is it logical? Is it both true and logical?

All Asians do well in college mathematics. Ikoto is an Asian. Therefore, she is good in mathematics.

This statement is logical but untrue. There is no contradiction in the premise and conclusion of the statement, but evidence does not support it. There are many Asian students who flop in college mathematics.

What Students Can Do to Acquire Thinking Skills

According to O'Day (1991) and Giarrusso *et al* (2001), students can develop critical thinking on their own when they know that thinking is about assessing the credibility of what they hear, read, and present; not accepting anything at its face value. O'Day (1991, p. 31) specifically stresses that learning to think critically appears more difficult than it really is. Students can develop thinking skills simply by asking simple questions of What? Where? When? Why? Who? and How? That is, in any communication or phenomenon they encounter students can think when they ask themselves, are these key questions adequately answered? The application of this idea about thinking is that students can think if they ask relevant questions when examining a) any phenomenon, issue or problem; and b) any communication.

Questions to stimulate thinking when examining a phenomenon, an issue or a problem:

- What is the pattern?
- When and where did the pattern emerge?
- Who is behind the pattern?
- How did the pattern emerge?
- Why did the pattern emerge?

Questions to stimulate thinking when examining communication:

- What is the purpose of the communication?
- Is the question or problem at issue clearly and precisely stated?
- What does the communication assume or take for granted? Is the assumption correct, reasonable?
- Are the key concepts of the communication clearly defined?
- What is the main idea/thesis/argument of the communication?
- What is the communicant's point of view? Is this point of view biased or neutral? Does it consider alternative points of view?
- Is the evidence relevant and adequate?
- How was the evidence collected?
- Is the interpretation of information reasonable?
- What explanation is provided? Is it convincing?
- Is there a problem with generalization?
- Does the conclusion flow from the discussion and the facts?
- What are the implications and consequences that flow from the conclusion?

Flowing from the above critical questions are the basic procedures for critical thinking about a text or presentation:

1. Identify the author's main purpose.
2. Figure out the main problems the author seeks to solve.
3. Discover the central question the author intends to answer.
4. Search for the main idea of the story.
5. Identify the main argument and the assumptions underlying it.
6. Identify the main concepts and how they are linked in the argument.
7. Spot the author's point of view.

8. Judge the adequacy and relevance of the evidence (data/information) to support the argument.
9. Find out if the key questions of who, what, when, where, why, and how are adequately answered.
10. Look for problems with overgeneralization.
11. Identify and assess the conclusions made.
12. Search for and evaluate the effects and implications of the conclusions.

Conclusion

Thinking produces originality, creativity, and innovation. Thinking is usually not stated in course outlines. However, it is a skill that is necessary for students to excel in academia. It is therefore important that students acquire the skill of thinking, particularly critical/analytical thinking. Like any other skills it takes effort, time, persistence, motivation, and practice to cultivate and effectively use thinking skills in education. Critical thinking is worth it. Pursue it with passion.

CHAPTER THIRTEEN

BECOMING A COMPETENT ACADEMIC READER

Introduction

Taking college/university courses involves reading lots of academic texts, and academic texts are puzzles to be solved. These make the need to acquire effective reading skills necessary.

In college/university super-speed techniques or reading substitutes of surveying or scanning and skimming are helpful steps to decide if the material deserves attention and thus worth reading. It is after reading reveals that the material deserves much more attention that a careful study is warranted. Studying is what academic reading is all about.

Lack of comprehension of academic texts stems basically from an inability to identify and understand the central question and the main thesis or line of argument the author is putting across, as well as the inability to critically assess the argument pursued in the text. The techniques of surveying, skimming, reading, scanning, and studying, if properly applied, can help break this intellectual barrier.

Techniques

Academic reading goes beyond the conventional wisdom of reading as surveying, skimming, scanning and mere reading of the text. Academic reading is about studying the text. Studying is reading for meaning or a deeper understanding of argument, and it requires higher level thinking. It is this type of reading that is called "Critical Reading," according to UNC-CH Writing Centre, 2006: www.unc.edu/depts/wcweb/handouts.

To Study:

- Read the material through non-stop
- Identify the central question
- Get at the main idea or thesis
- Reformulate the main and supporting ideas in your own words.
- Discover the underlying assumption
- Determine the purpose and implications
- Separate opinions from facts
- Notice the author's viewpoint

- Make inferences: reason something out from given evidence; a leap from the known to the unknown
- Reach conclusions: provide a logical finish
- Assess line of argument, evidence and logic
- Evaluate importance
- Question what you read: What central question is the author trying to answer? What is the main thesis or line of argument the author is proposing? What is the assumption behind this thesis? Does the author adequately defend his argument with evidence and logic? Does the author provide alternative argument and successfully refute it? Etc. (UNC-CH Writing Centre, 1998-2005: www.unc.edu/depts/wcweb/handouts).

Conclusion

Competent academic reading is about actively and relentlessly making sense of complicated texts. To facilitate comprehension, academic text must be surveyed and skimmed to identify its general structure, clues and signals to its basic ideas, and studied for a deeper meaning and critical evaluation. Thus, a competent reader is engaged in high level critical thinking while reading.

CHAPTER FOURTEEN

TAKING NOTES EFFECTIVELY AND EFFICIENTLY WHILE READING AND AT LECTURES

Introduction

A conversation between friends who are students:

Tomoko receives a low grade from a mid-term exam. Getting depressed she phones a friend, Fatima.

Tomoko: Hi Fatima, how are you doing?
Fatima: I am good. What about you?

Tomoko: I am very sad today.
Fatima: Why, any bad news from home?

Tomoko: No. I did poorly in my Sociology 101 mid-term exam.
Fatima: Sorry to hear that, what did you do wrong?

Tomoko: How come I take lots of notes and study them well for exams but do not do well?
Fatima: How do you take notes and how do you study them for exams?

Tomoko: I always try to write everything the teacher says, writes on the board, and puts on transparencies.
Fatima: I'm amazed at how you could copy everything coming from the teacher. How do you get the time to think and reflect on what the teacher presents when you are writing everything down?

Tomoko: I don't think in class, I take notes and memorize them as much as possible for exams.
Fatima: Hmmm, Tomoko, the way you take notes and study them might be the main problems for not doing well in exams. With the word-for-word copying of your teachers' presentations you are not likely to understand the course material and cannot properly answer questions that require some thinking. Moreover, with a large

amount of unprocessed notes, studying for exams becomes overwhelming, and when you are overwhelmed you cannot retain much information.

Tomoko: So Fatima, how do you take notes and study them?
Fatima: I am very selective in taking notes. I follow the teacher's presentation closely and write down, mostly in my own words only the important points the teacher raises. I differentiate among facts, concepts, descriptions, examples, stories, explanations, opinions, and conclusions of the presentation. I also reflect on how these parts of the presentation are related to each other. Where I am confused I ask questions for clarification before continuing with taking notes. In studying my notes for exams I make sure I understand the material. I memorize only the important facts and concepts.

Taking courses in the school system involves attending lectures and reading textbooks and journal articles for your sources of information. Since it is not practical to store the massive information generated by these processes in your mind, and since you need this information in preparation for your examinations, oral presentations and term papers, note taking is necessary. Given the necessity and value of note taking, as a student who aims at obtaining top grades, you need to develop effective techniques for taking notes from presentations, texts, and other forms of communication.

Types of Note Taking/Making

The literature on taking notes shows two major types of note taking. These are the verbatim technique and the selective technique. Although it is not the best, many students use the verbatim approach. As O'Day (1991, p.25) clearly concludes, "Most students write too much material using too many words." Some students even go to the extreme of writing down everything the professor says, shows, and/or writes "regardless of its significance or academic merit" (O'Day 1991, p.23). The verbatim approach to note taking stifles students' creativity. Specifically, the verbatim technique tends to prevent students from taking notes, thinking and assessing the lecture or text simultaneously. Thus it prevents mastery of course content and active learning. Given what has been said so far on this approach to note taking/making, it is clear that the verbatim technique is not recommended. For effective note taking then, the selective technique is more useful.

With the selective technique you are able to write down important information, think about, reflect on, review, and assess the information being presented to you all at the same time. In this way, you will be able to understand the course material and organization, and develop a useful, concise outline that will not be a mystery to you when you need to review the material for examinations, presentations, and/or term papers. It is a bad idea to merely use the highlighter to simply highlight texts; this encourages memorization and therefore prevents the attainment of the main goal of note taking—putting the ideas in the presentation in your own words (The UNC-CH Writing Centre (1998-2005: www.unc.edu/depts/wcweb/handouts).

This approach to note taking will help you organize ideas into manageable units and develop memory triggers that will facilitate learning and thus shorten review time for examinations and improve your grades. No wonder the selective technique is what productive students adopt.

Some Important Skills to Develop About Taking Notes

Note taking/making is an art as well as a science. You need to consciously and systematically learn it. The following are some useful suggestions O'Day (1991) and Giarrusso *et al* (2001) provide to help you in this direction.

1. Listen to the presentation and/or attentively with mental question marks (Why? When? What? Where? Who? How?) constantly remind yourself to assess the importance of what is being said:
   - How does what is being said right now fit into the overall structure of the presentation/argument?
   - Is what you are hearing now connected to what has just been said?
   - Anticipate where the professor/presenter is going with the presentation / argument.
   - Listen for signals of importance: lead-in phrases, key concepts, repetitions, changes in tone and emphasis in the professor's voice

2. Write down the main ideas or the meat or substance of the presentation rather than the presenter's flowery language.
   - Thesis
   - Argument
   - Explanation
   - Evidence
   - Conclusion

3. Outline the main points of the presentation/argument and the interconnections between the main points and evidence provided.

4. Politely ask the presenter to clear up anything in the presentation that confuses you.
   - Theories

- Concepts
- Phrases
- Issues
- Jargon

5. Leave spaces on your note page for your
   - Corrections
   - Comments
   - Additional note making when reviewing your notes.

6. Create a simple identification system for each note page to facilitate the re-sorting of your notes.
   - Lecture date
   - Abbreviated title of course and topic
   - Page number, etc.

7. Take notes in your own words. Quote (use quotation marks) the words/phrases/sentences of the presentation only when a paraphrase:
   - Would not capture the original meaning.
   - Would change the elegance effect of the original.

8. Develop and use your own note codes or a shorthand system to:
   - ➢ Distinguish between major and minor points of the presentation.
   - ➢ Differentiate among facts, opinions, examples, evidence, quotations, paraphrases, etc.
   - ➢ Write down information and ideas faster and correctly:
     - leave out unnecessary words: "and", "the", "but", etc.
     - leave out simple verbs: "is", "was", "went", "came", "be" etc.
     - use symbols to represent words: "=", "%", "#", "$", "&", "<", etc.
     - shorten words by:
       - shortening long words: "cont", "appr", "dev", "ex", etc.
       - using first syllable of a word: "org", "com", "edu", "pol" etc.
       - using first syllable and first letter of second syllable: "ind", "subj", etc.
       - using first syllable and add "s" for plurals and "g" for "ing": "chaps", "co-ops", "estg", "exptg", etc.
       - eliminating second syllable: "bio", "intro", "max", "rep", "chem.", etc.
       - using an apostrophe: "gov't", "am't", "cont'd", etc.
       - use a long phrase once and abbreviate when using it again:
         "Human Factor Competency" = "HFC"

9. Make notes talk to you by making important ideas jump out:
   - **Block** to emphasize key ideas and isolate memory cues
   - **Circle** to draw similar items together
   - **Arrow** to link ideas/thoughts together and/or connecting an item to additional item occurring out of sequence

10. Write the points down only once, and then:
    - Listen for elaboration
    - Clarification
    - Evidence
    - Examples
    - References

11. Read over your notes shortly after lectures/presentations to:
    - Make corrections
    - Clear up contradictions

Conclusion

Good note taking is a necessary skill all students need to acquire because it will help them stay alert in class, organize information into manageable units, remember important points of a presentation and text, shorten review time for examinations, and improve grades (O'Day 1991). Effective note taking skills can be developed by anyone once the process is broken into simple steps and conscious effort is made to master them. Like any other skill, it takes hard work and regular practice to hone note-taking skills (O'Day 1991).

CHAPTER FIFTEEN

BECOMING AN ACTIVE LEARNER: GROUP AND CLASS PARTICIPATION

Introduction

The Canadian academic culture expects that students verbally engage with the professor and class/group members. Yet many post-secondary students in Canada remain virtually silent in classrooms. The situation is worse in two cases. The first case applies to international students, refugees and new immigrants who usually come from an academic culture of silence in the school system in their home countries. The second case is with regard to Canadian minorities who don't speak in class because they are intimidated by the classroom as White space. Being silent in class and groups is interpreted as either you are not making sense of the course content/material and organization or you are not confident or both. Many professors perceive both behaviours as an indication of academic deficiency on the part of the student, and that may have a negative reflection on the student's grade. It is therefore imperative to be verbally active in your classes.

The Importance of Verbal Participation

Active class and group participation helps students to effectively capture and apply concepts, methodologies, and abstractions that are at the core of the academic system. In other words, people learn better and faster through action. Active learning improves students' grades. Moreover, many professors in the Canadian post-secondary education system expect active class participation from their students. In fact, class and group discussions are fast becoming major components of many courses offered in Canadian higher educational institutions.

Barriers to Active Verbal Participation:

The number one enemy of active verbal participation in class or group is fear. Students who fear that they will be ridiculed or devalued because their verbal contributions may fall short of the expected standards tend to be silent in class and groups. Underlying this fear are three main factors:

- Lack of knowledge

- Perceived language deficiency, especially accent in the case of international students, refugees and immigrants
- Low self-esteem

Another important barrier to active verbal participation is lack of interest. This occurs when the student perceives the course content and organization as irrelevant to his/her personal experiences, interests and goals.

Overcoming the Barriers: The Foundation of Active Verbal Participation

The fundamentals of active verbal participation are:

- Reading the course material before class
- Effective note taking/making
- Doing your fair share of the group project
- Ignoring the existence of other students in the class or group
- Assuming that the other students and professor would appreciate your contribution
- Resolving that you don't want other students to dominate the class or the group.

Reading Course Material Before Class

Students who competently read the course material before class may identify some confusion, contradictions, and difficulties with aspects of the reading material. This will help them generate pertinent questions that they can intelligently articulate in class because they have thought through the questions beforehand.

Taking Good Lecture Notes

Taking good notes in lectures also helps students to ask intelligent questions and answer questions intelligently. This is because using effective note taking skills such as a shorthand system; good page organization; distinguishing among major points, minor points, elaboration, examples; and having mental question marks during the lecture can give the student more time to think through the lecture and be critical. These are fertile grounds for generating questions and responding to questions from the lecture.

Doing Your Fair Share of the Group Project

One of the fundamental reasons why many students are passive in group discussion is lack of knowledge on the issues being discussed. A solution to this problem is doing your assigned portion of the group project. This will provide you with the knowledge base to contribute to discussions, make comments as well as ask intelligent questions and answer questions intelligently.

Ignore the Existence of Other Students

Nervousness, the negative emotional energy produced by perceiving people around you as significant others ready to ridicule you when you don't measure up to their standards, is a stumbling block to active verbal class or group participation. This barrier can be removed by redefining the situation either as those people do not exist or they are not better than you. Such redefinition may bolster your confidence level to express yourself in a group situation comfortably.

Relate Course Material and Lecture Content to your Personal Experiences and Goals

By looking at the lecture and course content from the perspectives of your personal life and goals, you can develop enough interest to motivate you to critically examine the material. In this way you will have questions to ask in class and can respond to questions with confidence.

Value of Sharing

The academic enterprise is a cooperative one. Your contribution matters. Conceiving that making your views and ideas accessible to your class members and professor will enrich the learning environment, and the course content will serve as good motivation to be verbally active in class.

Do Not Let Other Students Dominate the Class/Group

Resolving that you will not let other students dominate the class/group at your expense will compel you to contribute your quota in class or a group situation.

Consider the Cost of Education

Education in Canada is too expensive to remain passive in class.

Strategies for Successful Active Verbal Class Participation

From the discussion of the fundamentals of active verbal class and group participation, the following participation strategies can be derived:

- Ask intelligent questions.
- Answer questions intelligently.
- Make responsible comments.
- Do not dominate.

To be verbally active in class or group, you need to ask and answer questions. In order to earn respect and be taken seriously, your questions and answers should be intelligent ones. An intelligent question is one that addresses the perceived gaps and contradictions in the course material and lecture content. Likewise, an intelligent answer is one that directly responds to the core of the question posed. The skills of intelligent questioning and answering are developed from competent reading, critical thinking, and practice.

In some situations you may not have questions or be ready to respond to questions, but you may have some comments. Making comments is a way of being an active class/group participant. However, in order for your comments to enrich the class/group experience, they must be responsible ones. Responsible comments are based on the theme of the lecture, and are sensitive to the needs of the professor and class/group members.

Although you are expected to be verbally active in class, and being verbally active is beneficial, you should not be hyperactive. That is, do not dominate the class/group. In fact, to monopolize a class/group is to be insensitive to the rights of other students, and many students will stigmatize you for being dominant.

Conclusion

Interactive learning improves the learning capacity of students and improves their grades. Yet many students are passive in class and group situations because of fear and lack of interest. These problems can be countered with exposure to the benefits and strategies of active verbal participation. In your bid to be an active learner, however, be sensitive to the needs and rights of your professor and class/group members.

CHAPTER SIXTEEN

OVERCOMING THE FEAR OF ORAL PRESENTATIONS

An invited guest once wanted three volunteers in a school district to read out a skit she had prepared to illustrate a point in her presentation. To her surprise no students volunteered. Some post secondary students drop courses that have oral presentation components. The fact is, doing presentations of any kind in front of people is one of the scariest experiences for many people. Even seasoned public speakers confess that they get nervous about presentations. Some people experience knee jerking, shaky hands, and stomach upset when doing public presentations. In extreme cases some presenters pass out. Although many students literally hate oral presentations, oral presentation is increasingly becoming a part of many college and university courses. Scared about oral presentations or not, during your college/university years it is very likely you would occasionally have to present a prepared talk in front of a class. Students therefore need to develop the skills to overcome the fear of oral presentation and to give effective presentations.

Why So Many Students Are Scared of Oral Presentations

Most students are afraid of talking in front of their class because of one or more of the following reasons:

- Lack adequate knowledge about the topic
- Thoughts of embarrassment if they are unable to remember what they are supposed to say – going blank
- Expected criticisms from their classmates and professors
- Low grasp of the language of presentation
- Talking with non-mainstream accent

Signs of Bad Oral Presentations

- Reading all the presentation from a written script
- Repetitious
- Flat voice
- Low or Inaudible voice
- High pitch voice
- Talking too fast

- Making a speech
- Too many breaking sounds such as "ehe", "hmnn", "ers", "ems", etc.
- Going beyond allocated time
- Using too many transparencies or PowerPoint slides
- Using overcrowded transparencies or PowerPoint slides

How to Give Effective Oral Presentations

Adequate information about the topic, a good organization of the information into systematic structure, and rehearsal of the information and structure are the secrets to effective oral presentation. In a logical progression, according to O'Day (1991, p. 118):

- Introduce your presentation
- Discuss the main issues
- Draw relevant conclusions

Introducing Your Talk

This is the stage you provide an exciting preview of your talk to get the attention of the audience. It is therefore important that you clearly tell your audience exactly what you intend to do in the presentation and why. At this stage you highlight the central question and the main thesis of your presentation. Specifically, as O'Day (1991, p. 119) rightly advises,

- Give the title of your talk
- State what the purpose of your talk is
- Tell them what you will focus on, and if necessary what you will be leaving out
- List the points that you will be discussing
- Give any relevant background information to let the audience know why the topic is important

The Discussion Section of Your Talk

In this section you restate your thesis, that is, your line of argument and provide evidence to support it in such a way that the answer to your central question is given and a case for a final conclusion is made. The discussion section connects your introduction and conclusion with logical reasoning and relevant information or evidence. The evidence could be factual information, quotations, paraphrases, statistics, or a combination of them.

Concluding Your Talk

Many students make the mistake of thinking that a conclusion is a mere summary of the talk. The fact is, summarizing the main ideas of your presentation is a minor part of your conclusion. In fact, the conclusion section of your talk is an opportunity to bring closure to your talk in a way that would make a good impression on your audience. This is why you must:

- Concisely highlight the main idea in your discussion
- Emphasize your strong convictions about the issues you focus on and the answer you provide for the central question
- Relate the main point of your discussion to the bigger issues or theories in the topic area
- Ensure that your conclusion aligns with your thesis and evidence
- Sometimes you may use the conclusion to propose some new ideas or thoughts, but they must flow from your discussion section (O'Day 1991, p. 120).

Presentation Helpers

To prevent your presentation from becoming a boring speech, it is advised that students use audio-visual aids as oral presentation helpers (O'Day 1991). Until the invention of PowerPoint, many presenters used the black/white board, overheads, and handouts to supplement their oral presentations. Whatever presentation helpers you use, the principles that could guide you to make your presentation first rate include the following:

- use only key points
- use only a few names and dates
- speak to information in audiovisual aids; don't read them
- connect concepts with diagrams/charts
- use tables to represent statistical information
- use photos
- use very short audio or video clips

How to Present Your Talk: Reading, Rote or a Combination?

Reading: As much as possible avoid reading your prepared presentation. We agree with O'Day (1991, p. 120-121) when reading your talk from completely prepared text:

- Your talk seems cold and boring
- A mistake in the reading seems all the worse because it is all written down for you
- You lose your place or continuity when asked a question in the middle of your presentation
- Your audience get the impression you do not know your material

Rote: It is great to present your talk completely from memory as it creates the impression that you actually know your subject. However, as O'Day (1991, p. 120) correctly notes, only a few people have such a great memory. Many of us would forget many major points of our presentation and if we remember them at a later stage of the presentation and bring them up, it creates the impression that we are disorganized and incoherent.

Reading and Rote Combined: Effective oral presentations are the ones that avoid the two extremes and combination of reading written information and rote (O'Day 1991, p. 120). The use of quotations in oral presentation is effective when read or put on an overhead transparency or PowerPoint slide. Paraphrases and presenter's convictions present well using rote. PowerPoint or overhead transparencies are more effective in presenting statistical data, photos, graphical information, tables, charts and diagrams in an oral presentation. Cue cards with major points written on the front and elaborated on at the back are also a useful visual aid in oral presentations. Apart from sustaining audience attention, written information and other visual aids reduce presenter nervousness because when you get lost in the process of the presentation you could always resort to them and they can serve as safety nets.

Some Useful Tips for Successful Oral Presentations

The authors have come across the following useful tips in their attendance of and participation in numerous presentations around the world:

- Present your topic, main thesis and presentation outline or key concepts in written form: handout, handwriting on board, transparency, or PowerPoint slide.
- Direct the audience to what is on the handout, transparency, etc., but don't

read these materials to them.
- Stop and reorganize your thoughts when vital points in your presentation escape you or rephrase ideas when you think you were unclear.
- Wear comfortable and presentable clothing.
- Avoid mannerisms like touching your hair, making noise with keys or coins in your pocket, etc.
- Avoid jokes, sexist language, and racist language.
- Establish eye contact with audience and move around the room if possible.
- Don't overuse vocal inflections and hand gestures.
- Your voice must be clear and at the right volume: not too high and not too low.
- If you have a non-mainstream accent acknowledge it and speak slower; occasionally ask the audience if they follow your accent.
- Show confidence, and demonstrate enthusiasm in your subject.
- Keep the presentation simple.
- If you don't have an answer to a question, admit it.

CHAPTER SEVENTEEN

MASTERING ACADEMIC PRESENTATIONS: PROBLEM STATEMENT, CENTRAL QUESTION AND THESIS/HYPOTHESIS

Introduction

A professor was shocked when a full class diminished to about half on the second day of class. Her investigation revealed that many students had dropped the class mainly because the course outline stated that there would be student oral presentations and term papers. This seems to be a common occurrence in many post-secondary institutions in Canada. Some students drop courses that are not required when they discover that these courses involve term papers/research essays, reports and/or oral presentations. Many students, as much as possible, try to avoid courses that involve student presentations because they find the process of presentations difficult and uninteresting. Presentations are difficult for many people because they are ignorant of the important elements of good presentations. Once you discover that presentations are only about **Making a Clear Problem Statement**, asking specific **Questions** on relevant issues and providing contentious and factual answers (**Hypothesis/Thesis**) for them, presentations become interesting and less difficult.

Problem Statement

It is the same as stating the research problem. That is, an important flaw or deficiency in the existing knowledge about the topic you are focusing on. Resolving this flaw or bridging this gap in the knowledge is making a substantive contribution to existing knowledge. Formulating a good problem statement is therefore an exercise in originality, a very useful skill in both academia and life.

Central Question

Academic presentations revolve around asking thought-provoking questions and answering them with logical reasoning and factual information. In effect, the focus of presentations is a central question and a thesis statement or hypothesis. Discussions and arguments flow from this core. It is important to note that,

- In the academic world, whether you are reviewing a book/article, evaluating research/program/policy, describing an event, or explaining an issue, you must have a single clear and directly relevant question (Floyd 1995, p. 19).
- Even when the topic of study is posed in a question form you still need to come out with your own question derived from the original question (Floyd 1995, p. 19).

The main objective of a book, a book chapter, an article/paper, or a report is to provide an answer to a stated or unstated central question. Formulating a thesis or hypothesis is the beginning of pursuing that objective. In other words, a thesis or hypothesis is a brief proposed and provisional answer to a central question.

The central question is about making "your thoughts into a clear sentence that asks about the specific relationship between one or more factors" on a selected topic (Floyd 1995, p. 19). For example, the following could be a relevant central question on the topic "Leisure Among Canadian Racial Minorities": "What determines the major leisure activities of Canadian racial minorities?" It is important to note that there is more than one central question on any given topic. However, a good presentation requires only one central question. Moreover, the central question of a presentation may be implied or stated.

Uses of a central question: Richard Floyd (1995) correctly highlights the following uses of a central question in academic presentations:

- It helps you to personalize or take ownership of the project.
- It specifies the boundaries of the project.
- It narrows the focus of the project.
- It gives direction to the project.
- It promotes originality, innovativeness, and creativity.

Characteristics of a good central question:

- It has not been asked before (it is original).
- It prevents a simple yes or no answer.
- It specifies the relationship between two or more factors in the topic or statement of the research problem.
- It grabs attention and stimulates curiosity.

How to develop a good central question:

- Explore what interests you about the topic.
- Ask a few broad questions about the topic that relate to your interests.
- Select one of the questions that is most interesting to you.
- Write out your selected question and define its boundaries.
- Think and narrow the focus of your selected question.

Example:

Topic: Leisure and Canadian Racial/Ethnic Minorities.

Exploration of interests:

- How minorities perceive leisure.
- Leisure preferences of minorities.
- Leisure activities and experiences of minorities.
- The relationship between racism and leisure experiences of minorities.
- The relationship between traditional or non-western cultures and leisure preferences of minorities.
- Education and how minorities perceive leisure.

Broad Questions:

- How do minorities perceive leisure?
- What are the leisure preferences of minorities?
- What are the leisure activities and experiences of minorities in Canada?
- What is the relationship between racism and leisure experiences of minorities?
- What is the relationship between traditional cultures and leisure preferences of minorities?
- To what extent does formal education influence how minorities perceive leisure?

Selecting the Most Interesting Question to You:

- This is a matter of personal interest or experiences.
  - What is the relationship between traditional cultures and leisure preferences of minorities?

Specifying the Boundaries of the Question:

Traditional = Unique or sub-cultures of Canadian racial/ethnic minority groups
Leisure Preferences = Recreational activities minorities would like to participate in.
    Minorities = Non-Western European Groups.

Narrowing the Focus of the Question:

- To what extent do the unique cultures of non-Western Europeans in Canada influence their leisure travel preferences?

- **Exercise:** Create a central question from the topic "International students in Canada and home stay."

Thesis and Hypothesis

A presentation provides an answer to a central question, and the focal point of the answer is the thesis statement. A thesis in a research essay or term paper is the counterpart of the hypothesis of a quantitative research report (Giarrusso *et al* 2001, p. 143). A thesis statement, like a hypothesis, is usually a contentious/debatable claim or an assertion about a topic, that is, an answer to a central question that some would disagree with. For example, on the topic Leisure among Canadian Racial Minorities, a thesis statement may be, "The major leisure activities of Canadian racial minorities do not include traveling for pleasure." However, according to Northey and Tepperman (1993), a good thesis must go beyond a mere assertion. "Remember to be as specific as possible in creating a thesis, in order to focus your essay. Don't just make an assertion – give the main reason for it" (Northey and Tepperman 1993, pp. 12 and 13). In this case the above thesis must be changed to, "The major leisure activities of Canadian racial minorities don't include traveling for pleasure because of racism." Specifically,

- A thesis is a clear overall point/idea that is usually made up of an opinion and the main supporting reason(s) for that opinion in response to the central question asked about your topic.
- The thesis statement is the punch line of your argument.
- In short, a thesis is a brief, specific statement about a topic that may include or exclude supporting reason(s).

Characteristics of a good thesis/hypothesis: A good thesis/hypothesis:

- "Is narrow enough to be workable" (Northey and Tepperman 1993, p. 11).
- Creates "a line of argument for which you can supply adequate supporting evidence" (Northey and Tepperman 1993, p. 11).
- Has only one central idea.
- Goes beyond assertion (an assertion plus a reason).
- Avoids vague or ambiguous terms.

Uses of a thesis/hypothesis: The thesis serves as:

- A planning device that guides the collection and organization of information on a topic (Northey and Tepperman 1993, p. 13).
- A beacon towards which your project is steered (Floyd 1995, p. 25).
- A reference point for your argument (Floyd 1995, p. 25).

Creating a good working thesis/hypothesis:

> **Get a topic**:
>   - From academic literature, observations, and/or the mass media
>   e.g.: Gender and Cheating in Examinations

> **Create a central question**:
>   - Why do Canadian girls cheat more in examinations than Canadian boys? In the social sciences a central question is not answered with a simple "yes" and/or "no."

> **Form an opinion**:
>   - A thesis/hypothesis idea usually emerges as a response to a central question. For example, "Canadian girls cheat more in examinations than Canadian boys because of gender bias in the education system," could be an opinionated answer to the above central question.
>   - A thesis/hypothesis may also emerge from patterns, connections, or gaps you see in academic literature, observations, and/or the mass media.

> **Check your opinion against the essay topic**:
>   - If the opinion you have formed is relevant to the topic go to the next step below. If not re-examine your information and/or opinion.

> **Support your opinion:**
> - The reasons you give to support your opinion will not be anecdotes or individual details. Your reasons will usually refer to general categories or sub-categories.
> - You can make your supporting reasons more specific and precise when you revise your thesis in light of the material you gather and analyze.

e.g.: Canadian girls cheat more in examinations than Canadian boys because of the weaknesses of Canada's education system.

Refining your thesis:

> **Revise your thesis**: Your thesis needs revision if it:
> - **Merely restates the topic**: If the topic is "Gender and Cheating in Examinations," then "This essay will discuss gender and cheating in examinations" is a restatement of the topic, not a thesis.
> - **Merely states facts**: e.g. if you only summarize information on gender and cheating in examinations: Canadian girls cheat more in examinations than Canadian boys by smuggling exam answers into the exam room.
> - **Fails to provide supporting reasons**: e.g. Canadian girls cheat in examinations more than Canadian boys.
> - **Is the same as the thesis or theme of existing text or critics:** You will need to make a clear separation between your thesis and the overall point in any material you are examining.
> - **Fails to provide a structure for your essay**: a thesis often indicates the order of points to be discussed in the essay. e.g. Canadian girls cheat more in examinations than boys because of peer pressure, home problems, and weaknesses in the school system. The points "peer pressure," "home problems," and "weaknesses in the school system" will be the main order of points the essay will follow.
> - **Fails to reflect the body of your presentation**: a thesis must accurately reflect what you have said in the body of your essay. Therefore ensure that you change or modify your thesis to align with the body and conclusion of your essay.

> **Exercise:**
> - Is the following statement a thesis/hypothesis? Give reason(s) for your answer:

"All students have a specific teacher they claim as their favourite."

Conclusion

Academic presentations can be exciting and less difficult for you when you let your imagination go loose and generate questions of interest to you about the topic. With a clear STATEMENT OF A SIGNIFICANT PROBLEM, an insightful single question about the topic flowing from the problem statement, a hypothesis or thesis statement can be easily deduced which would provide a clear guide for gathering evidence and a linking logic for your argument or discussion. In essence, a solution to the presentation problem is personalizing the topic through a problem statement, central question and a hypothesis or thesis statement.

CHAPTER EIGHTEEN

CONSTRUCTING AN ARGUMENT: THE CENTER THAT HOLDS ACADEMIC PRESENTATION AND WRITING TOGETHER

Introduction

The lynchpin of term papers, research essays, research reports, research proposals, honour's and master's theses, doctoral dissertations, and oral presentations is ARGUMENT. Research, that is, data collection and data analysis, is to provide information to sustain an argument that presents a main thesis. In fact, argument is the litmus or acid test of presentations and writing. Unfortunately it is at the level of arguing the thesis that "many student papers (and some professional papers) falter" (Giarrusso *et al* 1994, p. 20). Such papers fail to coherently piece together thesis (the line of argument), reasoning, and evidence. Yet it is the ability to logically bridge the thesis and evidence that professors look for in grading student papers and reviewing peer manuscripts for publication. It is in this regard that academic presenters and writers need to pay particular attention to the argument of their papers. From the above comments, it could be deduced that an argument is about using evidence to logically defend a thesis. Floyd (1995, p. 42), clearly states that contrary to popular thinking

An argument does not need to have two or more people involved. It does, nonetheless, require that there be at least the potential for disagreement. In the social sciences, your argument must present evidence to support the position you have taken with your thesis statement.

Simply put, an argument is:

"…expressing a point of view on a subject and supporting it with evidence." (UNC-CH Writing Centre, 1998-2005: www.unc.edu/depts/wcweb/handouts)

- "In academic writing, an argument is usually a main idea, often called a 'claim' or 'thesis statement,' backed up with evidence that supports the idea." (UNC-CH Writing Centre, 1998-2005: www.unc.edu/depts/wcweb/handouts)

Essential Elements of an Argument

> ➢ Any good argument should have the following four elements:
>   - Logic: systematic reasoning connecting the premise and the conclusion
>   - Claim or premise: assertion or opinion
>   - Conclusion: the main idea that emerges from the reasoning and the premise
>   - Evidence: factual information, descriptions, explanations substantiating the claim and supporting the conclusion

A valid, sound, strong argument is one whose premises, reasoning, and evidence are all true and provide solid support for its conclusion; the conclusion does not go beyond the information contained in the premises (UNC-CH Writing Centre, 1998-2005: www.unc.edu/depts/wcweb/handouts), neither does the conclusion contradict the reasoning provided.

Types of Argument

- Deductive Argument
- Inductive Argument

Deductive Argument: A deductive argument moves from a general idea or theory to a particular instance. It is either valid or invalid. It is valid if both its premise and conclusion are true. It is invalid if the premise is true but the conclusion is false.

Examples:
a) *Valid Argument*: If all international students experience culture shock when they first come to Canada, then an international student in Canada experiences culture shock (TRUE). Kwasi has just come to Canada as an international student therefore he is experiencing culture shock (TRUE).

b) *Invalid Argument*: If all international students experience culture shock when they first come to Canada, then an international student in Canada experiences culture shock (TRUE). Kwame is not an international student in Canada (TRUE). Therefore Kwame is not experiencing culture shock (FALSE).
   - Although Kwame is not an international student, he may be a new immigrant or refugee in Canada and would therefore be experiencing culture shock.

Inductive Argument: This type of argument moves from a particular instance to a general idea or theory. It is either more or less sound. An inductive argument is sound if it is very likely that its conclusion is true given the information contained in the premise. It is less sound if it is less likely that its conclusion is true given the information contained in the premise.

Examples:

a) *A More Sound Argument*: Kwasi is experiencing culture shock (TRUE). Kwasi has just come to Canada to study as an international student and all international students experience culture shock in Canada (TRUE). Thus Kwasi is experiencing culture shock as all international students do in Canada (TRUE).

b) *A Less Sound Argument*: Kwasi is experiencing culture shock (TRUE). Kwasi has just come to Canada to study as an international student (TRUE). Thus Kwasi is experiencing culture shock as all international students do in Canada (MAY NOT BE TRUE).

- American students in Canada are international students but they may not experience culture shock because of the similarities between American and Canadian cultures.

Indicators of Argument

These words and phrases are used as signals to arguments. That is, an argument should contain one of these (or similar) words/phrases:

- Thus
- Therefore
- Hence
- This shows that
- This suggests that
- Consequently
- So
- Accordingly
- This implies that
- This proves that

The Necessity of Counterargument in a Good, Strong Argument

- For the argument to be good, it must be persuasive. That is, it must argue both in favour of the main claim of the thesis and against the best alternative claims (Northey and Tepperman 1986/1993).

In other words, "an important way [besides acceptable evidence] to strengthen your argument and show that you have a deep understanding of the issue you are discussing is to anticipate and address counterarguments or objections" (UNC-CH Writing Centre, 1998-2005: www.unc.edu/depts/wcweb/handouts).

Counterarguments are what the existing knowledge that disagrees with your view would say about the premises and conclusion of your argument. The academic way of identifying counterarguments to your argument is the review of existing literature or knowledge.

What do you do with counterarguments once they are identified? The UNC-CH Writing Centre handouts (2006), correctly point out that in order to produce a good, strong argument you need to acknowledge one or two serious identified counterarguments and respond to them in some depth, rather than to provide superficial replies to a list of counterarguments. This handout wisely cautions against caricaturing or being simplistic about counterarguments. It advises one to be generous in presenting the counterarguments. That is, counterarguments must be presented "fairly and objectively, rather than trying to make it look foolish…or simply attacking or caricaturing your opponents" (Ibid.). You could effectively respond to counterarguments by a) conceding that the counterarguments are valid but explaining why your argument should nonetheless be accepted or b) rejecting the counterarguments and showing why they are mistaken (Ibid.). However, "if considering a counterargument changes your position, you will need to go back and revise your original argument accordingly" (UNC-CH Writing Centre, 1998-2005: www.unc.edu/depts/wcweb/handouts).

How to Develop a Good Argument

1. Clearly state your central questions and related questions.
2. Clearly state your thesis (provisional answer to your central question).
3. Separate the thesis into its "claim" and "conclusion" parts.
4. Examine the evidence you have collected for pieces that coherently connect the two parts of the thesis.
5. Use each part of this evidence to develop discussion sections of the paper: they should help provide reasoning for why the point is true and explain the logical linkage between that point and the main claim of the thesis.

6. Examine the evidence for pieces that permit alternative arguments or counterarguments, and see how they could be used to modify and strengthen your argument.
7. Strive for scientific truthfulness: remain unbiased and unemotional. That is, do not make emotional appeals to decency and morality, for "they count for nothing in a logical argument" (Northey and Tepperman 1993, p. 100).
8. Discuss evidence that does not fit.
9. Keep it simple: "Strive for elegant simplicity, bold reasoning, and clean data: this is the social scientist's [the scholar's] motto" (Northey and Tepperman 1993, p. 103).

Example:

The following is an abstract of a published article from one of the authors that fairly illustrates the development of a good argument. The title is "Globalization and Diversity in the Tourism Industry: A Human Factor Perspective" Review of Human Factor Studies, Special Issue. Volume 8 (1): 49-73.

At the interface of globalization and tourism is a natural diversity in the areas of demographic and cultural representations. However, the tourism industry tends to push this diversity to the margins with the assumption that cultural cloning at the core of the industry would maximize the bottom-line. This paper argues that this assumption is faulty. It agrees with postmodern thinking that tourism can optimize productivity/profit, enhance social justice, enrich cultures, and motivate environmental conservation when it facilitates rather than destroys diversity. It also affirms the postmodernist position that diversity can be successfully facilitated in tourism in spite of the homogenizing tendencies of globalization. However, contrary to the perspective of postmodernism, this paper does not problematize globalization. This is because globalization is not the problem. The problem is human factor decay and/or underdevelopment. Therefore, the key to successful facilitation of diversity in tourism is not the halting of globalization and/or multiculturalism policies and diversity management as many postmodernists believe, but rather the application of appropriate human factor.

The Importance of Evidence in Arguments

Without evidence an argument stays only as a thesis or hypothesis, that is, a claim without substance remains as a mere opinion. This is arrestingly captured by the statement that "the strength of your evidence, and how you use it, can make or break your argument" (UNC-CH Writing Centre, 1998-2005: www.unc.edu/depts/wcweb/

handouts). In academia, acceptable evidence is what is termed "empirical evidence" or factual information. That is, evidence produced by systematic scientific research.

Acceptable evidence is diverse and emerges from various sources. In disciplines such as the physical sciences and some specializations of psychology hard facts are what is acceptable as evidence. This is the evidence produced through experiments and detached or objective observations. The other social sciences, humanities and business fields recognize statistics produced from social surveys, narratives and case studies produced through participant observations and interviews, factual information created out of content analysis of text, stories, plays, physical traces, photographs, artwork, craft, audios, videos, etc., as credible evidence to back up arguments.

CHAPTER NINETEEN

GOING BEYOND ACADEMIC ARGUMENT: PROVIDING AN EXPLANATION

Introduction

Students doing a group project on housing problems of new immigrants, refugees and Aboriginals hypothesized that a central registry of housing would assist needy families in this category to find temporary homes. The hypothesis neglects how the registry could assist. Another group of students proposed that people from minority and majority racial groups in North America use racist words differently. Like the first group they failed to provide an answer to the "why" question. The fact is, a presentation that addresses "how" and "why" issues should go beyond an argument. It should contain an explanation. All good essays or papers connect the central question, thesis, argument, and explanation.

Explanation

➢ It is an argument that accounts for how and/or why something happens. That is, aligning the thesis and evidence to account for something (Moore and Parker 1995). In effect, an explanation goes beyond an argument.

➢ e.g. Rei and Rena discussing whether or not Rena's friend is brilliant:

- Rei: "Look, Rena, I told you your friend is not brilliant. Look how he is struggling with Economics 101".

- Rei has just given an argument *that* Rena's friend is not brilliant. The issue here is *whether* Rena's friend is brilliant or not, and Rei has advanced an *argument* that Rena's friend is not brilliant.

- But let's suppose that Rei and Rena *agree* that Rena's friend is not brilliant. That is, the issue of whether Rena's friend is brilliant or not is settled. Rei and Rena might then consider a further issue of *why is it* that Rena's friend is not brilliant. Rei then might say: "The reason Rena's friend is not brilliant is because he eats too much junk food." In this case Rei has given an *explanation* of why Rena's friend is not brilliant.

- If we try to settle *whether or not a thesis (viewpoint) is valid or sound,* we give an **argument**. If, instead, we try to *show what makes a thesis (viewpoint) valid or sound,* then we propose an **explanation**. In short, unlike an argument, an explanation sheds light on the *cause(s)* of something.

- While an argument tries to sustain or support a thesis (a viewpoint), an explanation can be entirely neutral; it does not judge (approve or disapprove) something.

Characteristics of a Good Explanation

➢ A good explanation should be persuasive or convincing, and to be persuasive it should be testable, non-circular, relevant, specific, able to explain more things, and stronger than alternative explanations (Moore and Parker 1995, pp. 201-206):

- **Testable:** There should be a way to find out if it is correct or incorrect.
  > e.g.: *Poor Francis! Why did he die at such a young age? I guess it was due to fate.*

  "Fate" is not a good explanation because there is no way that you can verify fate and test its effect on peoples' lives. On the other hand, if the explanation was that Francis died so young because of poor diet, this could be systematically tested.

- **Non-circular:** Not merely restating the thing it is intended to explain, nor should it merely describe the thing in different words.
  > e.g.: *Mika sits at the computer but she simply cannot think of anything to write. It's because she has writer's block.*

  Writer's block is only another way of saying one cannot think of anything worthy of writing. A non-circular explanation would be that Mika cannot think of anything to write because she is homesick.

- **Relevant:** Allows us to predict the thing it explains with some degree of confidence.
  > e.g.: *Mayuko wishes to explain why Piyaporn always orders peppermint at the ice cream shop, and she says that Piyaporn is allergic to chocolate.*

  Being allergic to chocolate does not mean that you cannot eat any other flavour of ice cream but peppermint. Having a chocolate allergy does not predict that you will choose peppermint.

- **Specific:** Not vague or too broad.

  > e.g.: *Sandy is rude on the phone, and Ikoto asks another friend why. She is told that Sandy is having a bad day.*

  "Bad day" can mean so many things. Specify what it is that has made Sandy's day a bad one. It could be she has failed a major exam.

- **Reliable:** If an explanation leads to prediction that turns out to be false, then it is unreliable.

  > e.g.: *The lights go out in your classroom. Someone explains that British Columbia Hydro Corporation has suffered a power failure. Looking out the window, however, you notice that lights are on in other classrooms in your block.*

  It cannot therefore be true that the electricity corporation has experienced a power failure. If it is so all lights on campus would be out.

- **Explain more things**, especially when the explanation comes in a form of a theory.

  > e.g.: *There were two racial minority groups living in Canada who have high educational qualifications.*

  Sociologist A comes up with a theory that explains what may have happened to one of the minority groups, but this theory is irrelevant to the other minority group. Sociologist B comes up with a theory that explains what may have motivated the two groups towards higher education. Theory B has more explan-atory power.

- **Absence of alternative explanations**: Provides a better explanation than existing or alternative explanations.

  > e.g.: *Racial minorities score low on standard tests because these tests focus on mainstream cultural knowledge.*

  This is a stronger explanation than the alternative that racial minorities' low test scores are due to their small brains.

CHAPTER TWENTY

RESEARCH:
COLLECTING DATA TO PRODUCE EVIDENCE

Introduction

Without solid empirical evidence, that is, factual information, the thesis of your research essay or term paper remains a mere opinion and the hypothesis for your research report cannot be tested. Argument breaks down without acceptable evidence. Factual information helps transform a thesis from an opinion to an argument or translates hypothesis from a mere guess into a confirmed or disproved theory. Reliable and valid evidence is obtained through scientific research designs/methods and techniques. The research question or thesis/hypothesis dictates the type of evidence collected, and the research design/methods and techniques determine the quality of evidence obtained. There are two main sources of evidence, firsthand (primary) data and second hand (secondary) data.

Illustration:

Research Question: What is the difference between the educational attainments of White Canadians and Canadians of Colour, and why?

Thesis/Hypothesis: Canadians of Colour have higher educational qualifications than White Canadians because of differences in their cultural expectations.

Evidence needed to support this thesis or test the hypothesis: There are two main variables or factors in this thesis/hypothesis that need information/data
1. Variable or Factor #1: Educational Qualifications
    Information/Data needed: Statistics of educational qualifications of the two groups
2. Variable or Factor #2: Cultural Expectations
    Information/Data needed: Documented and observed evidence and/or perceptions of cultural expectations of the two groups

Sources of information/data on variable #1:
a) Statistics Canada's publications on educational qualifications of Canadians.

b) Books, journal articles and dissertations that have compiled tables on educational qualifications of Canadians.
- These sources are secondary and therefore produce SECONDARY DATA.

Sources of information on variable #2:
a) Books, journal articles, and dissertations on mainstream cultures, subcultures, and countercultures of Canadian society.
b) Social survey results of a scientific sample of Canadians completing questionnaires on cultural expectations.
c) Interview results of a selected sample of Canadians on cultural expectations.
- Source a) is SECONDARY DATA, while sources b) and c) are PRIMARY DATA.

d) Results of observed cultural expectations.

It is important to note that in the education system the sources of information that are trusted or have most credibility are academic sources of secondary data and systematically/scientifically collected primary data (Floyd 1995). Non-academic sources or subjective information or opinions are not acceptable as good data (Floyd 1995). Floyd (1995) also insightfully points out that the acceptable forms of data can be classified into:

- Facts: statistics and arguments or research findings of credible scholars.
- Descriptions: information stating the characteristics of something as a matter of fact.
- Explanations: Theories.

Secondary Data

Information collected and published/presented by other researchers for purposes different from your own research.

Sources:
1. Academic:
- Refereed journals
- Papers presented at academic conferences
- Honour's, Master's, and Doctoral dissertations
- Books with exhaustive citations for information that is well researched.
- Official statistics

-These sources are the foundation upon which any credible description and\or explanation is based because they have been screened for scholarly value.

2. Nonacademic:
   - Popular print: newspapers and magazines
   - Broadcast media: television and radio
   - Anecdotes: personal observations, information from friends, relatives, etc.

-These sources are useful mainly for exploring your topic because they are either screened only for their entertainment value or they were not systematically collected and analyzed.

How to obtain secondary data: Prominent scholars/researchers on this issue such as Floyd (1995) and Northey and Tepperman (1993) would advise that you:

- Scan the references of the required and recommended texts provided in your course outline for specific sources of relevant information.
- Type the key words and phrases of your research topic into a library terminal to develop a list of possible sources relevant to your topic.
- Put together a list of major words or concepts in your research topic and give it to your librarian for assistance.
- Ask your librarian to help you with information about available CD-ROMs that may contain information relevant to your research topic.
- Find the major names in the field for your research topic and use the Internet to obtain their e-mail addresses. Ask them for help to access relevant information.
- Search community, district, and university libraries for additional resources. Depending on your research topic, you may also consult archives and libraries of government departments, corporations, and companies.
- Use your imagination, planning, and courtesy, and be clear on the focus and purpose of your study.

Keeping record of your search for secondary data:

- Make notes on the main ideas, arguments, descriptions, explanations, opinions, and facts.
- Record citations or references for all the information you gather.

Primary Data: Information from original sources

Types of primary data and how to obtain them:

1. Quantitative Primary Data:

   ➢ Information in numerical form that enables researchers to apply statistical methods used in the natural and physical sciences. This information is more precise, but sometimes less true to life.
      - Survey research: Use questionnaires to gather information from a large sample of people.
      - Experimental research: Observe or ask questions for responses after something new is introduced to a situation or group of people.
      - Collecting artifacts: Arts, crafts, archaeological remains, bones, photographs, letters, memos, diaries, minutes, magazines, commission reports, novels, speeches, essays, parliamentary debates, etc.

2. Qualitative Primary Data:

   ➢ Information in the form of words that are true to life, but less precise.
      - Interviews: Asking people prepared questions relevant to your research for their responses.
      - Detached observation: Observing something systematically with your eyes without talking to the observed and participating in the activities of the observed.
      - Participant observation: Observing something while at the same time talking to and participating in the activities of the observed.

3. A combination of Quantitative and Qualitative Data:

   (a) Reducing verbal information into numeric information for generalization; content analysis
   (b) Interpreting numeric information from the point of view of survey respondents or participants in experiments. Non-technical inferences.

Recording Primary Data

- Circle or cross the codes of chosen answers on questionnaires.
- Write down or indicate electronically the codes respondents select in telephone interviews.

- Write notes on interviews and observations.
- Audiotape or videotape interviews.
- Videotape observations.
- Photograph or videotape arts, crafts, and archaeological remains.
- Photocopy or take notes on archival material and other print texts.

Avoiding the Frequent Pitfalls of Data Collection

Many researchers face the problem of collecting irrelevant information and not knowing when to stop data collection. To avoid these problems, Floyd (1995) rightly suggests that you:

1. **Keep your goal in focus:**
   > Write what you are researching and keep it in front of you
   - Thesis or Hypothesis
   - Main concepts or variables or factors

2. **Be strict or critical in assessing information:**
   - Don't include information items that are not relevant to your thesis, hypothesis or main concepts.
   - Keep the information items that contribute in a big way to supporting your thesis/hypothesis.
   - Keep the information items that contradict your thesis/hypothesis.
   - Don't keep opinions; rather, keep relevant facts, descriptions, and explanations.

3. **Know when to stop data collection:**
   - Stop data collection when you are not getting any new information relevant to your thesis/hypothesis.

CHAPTER TWENTY-ONE

RESEARCH:
ANALYZING AND INTERPRETING DATA TO PRODUCE EVIDENCE

Introduction

After collecting a massive amount of information about your research problem what do you do with it?

The most overwhelming stage of the research process to many research students is data analysis. Some students quit the research at this stage. Data analysis, however, shouldn't necessarily be a daunting task, if you know the questions to ask about the data (Northey and Tepperman 1993). After gathering enough information, facts, descriptions, and theories for your term paper or thesis project, there is the need to analyze this information for underlying themes and patterns. Data analysis in the social sciences involves classifying, identifying, assigning, arranging, and relating collected information to discover themes and patterns to make an argument out of a thesis to provide a convincing answer to the research question (Northey and Tepperman 1993).

- **Analyze it:** discover themes and patterns in the data.
- **Interpret it:** make sense/meaning of the data; crack the shell of the data to reveal the meaning within.

It is important to know that data analysis aims at providing correct answers to the following pertinent question:

- What do the data say? or specifically
- What message is/are the voice(s) of the data communicating? or
- What themes and patterns stand out from the data?

The analysis may be done manually or by using computer software.

ANALYSIS = Examining information/data for themes and/or patterns
INTERPRETATION = Examining themes and/or patterns revealed by data analysis for meanings

Processes of Data Analysis

a) It begins with classification:
   ➢ Classify the secondary information into:
      • Facts
      • Descriptions
      • Explanations

   ➢ Classify the primary information into:
      • Qualitative
      • Quantitative

   ➢ Classify information sources into:
      • Quotations
      • Paraphrases
      • Journal articles
      • Internet discussions
      • Books
      • Interviews
      • Observations

b) After classification comes identification:
   ➢ Identify the various classifications with:
      • Letters,
      • Numbers, or
      • Colours

c) Assignment follows identification:
   ➢ Assign appropriate information to:
      • The variables on concepts of your thesis
      • The various sections of the paper:
         ▪ Introduction
         ▪ Argument
         ▪ Conclusion
         ▪ References

d) When assignment is complete, arrangement begins:
   ➢ Arrange the various items of information under each:
      • Variables or concepts of the thesis
      • Section of the paper in their order of presentation:

- First, second, third, etc., item to be presented in the introduction.
- First, second, third, etc., item to be presented in the body/argument/explanation.
- First, second, third, etc., item to be presented in the conclusion.

e) The last stage in data analysis is relating the items of information to the various parts of the thesis. This involves:
  - Deciding on how the various items of information support your thesis:
    - If an item provides strong support, keep it.
    - If it is not clear where an item fits in the thesis, throw it out.

  - Showing the implication of each item for your thesis:
    - Does it confirm your thesis?
    - Does it contradict your thesis?
    - Does it permit alternative arguments?
    - Does it permit logical reasoning?
    - Does it allow unbiased and unemotional argument?

  - Developing a general conclusion about the data in relationship to your thesis:
    - Draw a conclusion or a set of conclusions from analyzing the various items of information as to their overall strength in helping to coordinate a convincing argument in support of the thesis.

  Overall, data analysis is about allowing the data to speak for itself, unlike in data interpretation where the researcher speaks for the data.

  - The general principle guiding data analysis is:
    - Look carefully, inquiringly, and critically at the data. A good researcher overlooks nothing.

Data Interpretation

"Very few facts are able to tell their own story, without comments to bring out their meaning" (John Stuart Mill 1859: quoted in Northey and Tepperman 1986, p. 91). The fact is data analysis reveals factual patterns. However, as Northey and Tepperman (1986, p. 90) correctly observed,

...the meaning of any fact [pattern] is not self-evident... Is the glass half-empty or half-full? No facts can answer this question. Facts say only how much is in the glass: the rest is interpretation… Facts do not speak for themselves; they always need interpreting.

The point is, interpretation is what gives meaning to facts/patterns. In effect, data analysis is about using open-mindedness, imagination, and appropriate tools to find THEMES and PATTERNS in the data, while data interpretation is about inferring MEANINGS from the themes and patterns:

- **Qualitative Data Analysis:** Finding themes and patterns in textual/verbal/visual data. It is about using inductive reasoning to sort and categorize empirical textual/ verbal with the objective of discovering the abstract, underlying themes and patterns of the information. Computer software programs such as DataEase, Ethnograph, Filemaker Pro, HyperQual, HyperRESEARCH, NUD*IST, Invivo, and QualPro can facilitate the process.

- **Qualitative Data Interpretation:** Inferring meanings from the themes and patterns in textual/verbal/visual data and stating the logical and practical implications of the meanings beyond the specific case of your research.

- **Quantitative Data Analysis:** Finding patterns in numerical data. It is a process of organizing, summarizing, and examining numerical data for patterns and meanings by using statistics and electronic spreadsheet computer programs. Statistical software packages such as SAS, SPSS, SYSTAT, Minitab, StatView, and Statistica are very handy in analyzing quantitative data. The data analysis process involves identifying the following features of the data: characteristics, distribution patterns, associations and relationships.

- **Quantitative Data Interpretation:** Inferring meanings from the patterns in the statistical outputs resulting from the examination of the numerical data, relating the meanings to the research problem/question, and stating the logical and practical implications of meanings beyond the specific case of your research.

Conclusion

Data analysis and interpretation can be tedious and time consuming. However, they are important stages in constructing a term paper, research report/essay, and thesis/dissertation report. This is because data analysis and interpretation help to determine if information collected is good enough or adequate to make a valid and sound argument from the thesis/hypothesis to answer the research question. If the pieces of evidence collected prove to be a solid basis for the argument, begin the write-up. If not, find the relevant information to fill in the gaps.

CHAPTER TWENTY-TWO

CREATING THE INTRODUCTION AND CONCLUSION FOR YOUR PRESENTATIONS AND PAPERS

Introduction

An introduction is like the front yard or the main entrance or door to a house. It gives the first impression of the presentation. If it is not thoughtfully done it puts off the audience. Being the gateway to the presentation, an introduction either makes or mars the rest of the presentation. The introduction, like a steering wheel of a vehicle, determines the focus of the presentation and guides it. Many students know that the introduction is the beginning part of a presentation that introduces it. However, they do not know exactly what should go into the introduction.

- What is the content of a good introduction?

Giarrusso *et al*'s (2001, pp. 18 and 20) answer to this nagging question is very helpful. According to them, the *introduction:*

1. Presents the question [stated or unstated] that is being answered and the general claim or thesis/hypothesis of the presentation.
2. Specifies the plan for answering the question and/or arguing the thesis.
3. Summarizes what other people have written about the topic and shows why it is still an important issue to study. In other words, the introduction should state your position on the issue in the context of the positions of other scholars.
4. Is original, creative, relevant and catchy.

An Example of a Good Introduction

The following introduction was first published as the introduction of "Francis Adu-Febiri, (2002). Globalization and Diversity in the Tourism Industry: A Human Factor Perspective." Review of Human Factor Studies, Special Issue. Volume 8 (1): 49-73.

Topic: Globalization and Diversity in the Tourism Industry

The irony is that the very globalization that threatens cultural diversity also bolsters cultural diversity by facilitating immigration and promoting a greater desire to be special or claim differences in the midst of mass consumerism. The most crucial question is whether or not the diversity resulting from globalization can be used for the benefit of all rather than just a few. This paper agrees with the postmodernists that diversity can be used for the benefit of all but disagrees with the position of these theorists that globalization is the problem and official multiculturalism is the way to make diversity work for society. Globalization is not necessarily a problem. Globalization works against diversity in postmodern society mainly because of human factor deficiency. Therefore a multiculturalism policy cannot make diversity work for the tourism industry. The results of attempts to implement multiculturalism policies in countries such as Canada, Australia, and Singapore show the multiculturalism policies freeze cultural diversity in time and push it into the margins of communities, institutions, and organizations. It is in light of the poor track record of the attempts to make multiculturalism work for diversity that this paper proposes a new diversity model, "Facilitating Diversity Model." This new model claims that the key to putting diversity to work for the tourism industry is the application of appropriate human factor in the form of human factor competency.

To support this claim, section one of the paper explores diversity dynamics of tourism in the context of globalization. Section two looks at the multiculturalism model of diversity in the tourism industry. In section three the "Facilitating Diversity Model" is introduced. It is used to show how and why globalization-produced diversity in the tourism industry could be used to increase profits, improve tourist-host relationships, and benefit the economies, cultures, and environments of destination communities. The concluding section re-emphasizes the interconnections among globalization, diversity in the tourism industry, and the human factor. It highlights that human factor competency is the key to make diversity work for all in a globalized world.

What is a Conclusion?

Many students often find it difficult to draw a conclusion for their presentations because they think that they have already said all that they can say about the topic. Conclusions should not necessarily be difficult when you know what a conclusion is.

1. A conclusion is a decision, an opinion or an idea you come to after looking at a situation and thinking about it (O'Day 1991).
2. A conclusion summarizes the overall argument and offers the author's concise personal thoughts about the issue presented (Giarrusso *et al* 2001).

Characteristics of a Good Conclusion

1. It should flow from the argument.
2. It should be based on the evidence cited to support the argument.
3. It should be a concise interpretation of the argument.
4. It should provide a fresh summary statement of the argument.
5. It should go beyond a mere summary to provide insight into the main issue the argument focuses on.
6. It should relate the argument to the general debates on the topic.
7. It should close with the personal thoughts about the issue the author discusses in the presentation (Giarrusso *et al* 2001, p. 20).

Where Do You Get Fresh Ideas to Conclude Your Presentation?

➤ Look into your introduction and body of your presentation:
  • Don't use the same words to restate your thesis and don't change its meaning.
  • Don't use the same words to highlight your argument and explanation.
  • Don't just summarize what is in your essay/paper by listing them.
  • Don't bring in any new ideas.

An Example of a Good Conclusion

The following conclusion was first published as the conclusion of "Francis Adu-Febiri, (2002). Globalization and Diversity in the Tourism Industry: A Human Factor Perspective." Review of Human Factor Studies, Special Issue. Volume 8 (1): 49-73.

Topic: Globalization and Diversity in the Tourism Industry

Tourism as an important part of globalization does not necessarily destroy diversity as postmodernists believe. The main destroyer of diversity is human factor deficiency or decay. The postmodernist approach to maintain cultural diversity through the halting of globalization and official multiculturalism, is therefore flawed. The global integration of societies and communities is so powerful that it is unlikely to be stopped. It is not even necessary to halt the process because globalization is not the problem. Globalization merely reinforces existing domination systems and inequalities resulting from human factor deficiencies.

It is in this light that the facilitating diversity model is important. This model offers hope for a more effective direction to productive diversity in the tourism industry because it focuses on the development of human factor competency. Since the existing barriers to productive diversity in tourism are the symptoms of human factor decay, cultural competency programs that postmodernists endorse could not change the tourism industry to work for diversity. Therefore if the tourism industry is serious about diversification that works for the benefits of all, it needs to channel adequate resources to the development and application of human factor competency among tourism entrepreneurs, managers, and employees.

Chapter Twenty-Three

Producing A+ Term Papers and Research Essays: Tricks of the Trade

Introduction

Another nightmare of many post-secondary students is writing term papers (based on library information) or research essays (based on primary information). This is because writing a term paper/research essay requires students to describe/examine/ discuss/explain a complex original idea with relevant information in a way that makes it understandable and convincing, a skill/knowledge form that many students lack. Writing itself is not the main problem. Lack of academic originality and creativity and knowledge is the problem. Students are so used to situations where teachers identify problems to solve or ideas to work with that it is hard for them to think of original ideas or identify problems and solve them creatively. Moreover many students do not have adequate knowledge about the structure, main components, and contents of the components of a good term paper/research essay. Writing papers/ essays is fun if:

- You have a central question and thesis/hypothesis that are original.
- You know how to collect, analyze and interpret relevant information.
- You know how to creatively put an argument together.
- You know the form and parts of a good paper/essay and what goes into its various parts.

Grammar, spelling and expressions could be taken care of by an editor. Yet, many existing books on term paper or research essay writing focus on the "writing" process. These books highlight writing skills such as:

1. Writing at your level of comfort.
2. Writing clearly.
3. Free writing first and editing later.
4. Using headings and subheadings.
5. Sketching introductions and conclusions.
6. Referencing and citation styles.

In short, the literature tends to focus on the technicalities or style of writing term papers and research essays at the expense of the substance of papers/essays. The fact is, teachers give more marks for substance than style. In this light, although this chapter does not neglect style it puts more emphasis on substance of term papers and research essays. The main difference between a term paper and research essay is the source of data or evidence. Term papers utilize secondary or existing (usually published) information, whereas research essays utilize primary or firsthand information.

The Substance of Writing Term Papers and Research Essays

1. **Originality:** Being original means that your central question or thesis/hypothesis is not addressed in the literature on the topic of your essay. To have an original question or thesis/hypothesis, you need to explore your personal experiences or observations about the issues involved in the topic. Create *who, where, when, what, how and why* questions based on your experiences/observations and explore the literature to find out to what extent it answers your questions. The question least answered in the literature will provide an original question for your paper/essay. A thesis/hypothesis developed from this question is original. Northey and Tepperman (1986, p. 112) insightfully suggest that "*How* and *why* questions are often most productive, since they take you beyond information-gathering and force you to analyze and interpret."

Example:

As a minority in Canada, if in your travels to tourist attractions/destinations you don't see other minorities vacationing, you may have questions such as:

- How do Canadian minorities spend their leisure time if they have any?
- To what extent do Canadian minorities travel for pleasure?
- Why don't many Canadian minorities participate in leisure travel?

With these questions in mind, you begin to explore or skim the literature (not commentaries) on leisure travel among Canadians to see if these questions are adequately answered or not. If they are not you have an original question from which you can create an original thesis/hypothesis for your term paper or research essay.

2. **Creativity in Collecting and Processing Evidence:** The type of evidence you collect, how you collect it, how you analyze the evidence, and your interpretation of the evidence all contribute in a large way to the quality of your term paper/research essay. Creativity is the key to successfully collecting, analyzing, and interpreting evidence for your term paper/research essay. To start with, the

evidence you need for your paper/essay is determined by the major factors or variables in the claim part and the conclusion part of your line of argument. The line of argument in term papers requires secondary sources of evidence; that is, evidence from existing literature on the topic. Library material, Internet information, official statistics, and/or archival material provide adequate evidence for a term paper. It does not require much creativity to access this type of information. However, it requires that you come up with creative categories and themes to process the information for your argument. Unlike term papers, research essays usually require primary information. This information is obtained from observations, questionnaire surveys, interviews, and/or artifacts. This type of information is more difficult to collect since it involves dealing directly with people. It takes a lot of planning, time, money, and emotional investment. In some extreme situations you may have to deceive and/or risk your life in order to get genuine information. The ethical problems are difficult to deal with. Moreover, the processing of primary data is less straightforward and neat. You therefore need to be very creative if you are to produce trusted evidence from this source. The good news is that there is a lot of information available in research method books on how to successfully collect primary data and deal with the ethical challenges involved.

3. **Knowledge:** One of the main difficulties many students encounter in producing term paper/research essay is their lack of knowledge about the structural contents of a good paper/essay. Many students know that a term paper/research essay should have an introduction, a body, a conclusion, and citation. However, they do not know what exactly goes into these individual components.

The introduction states the main idea (a single-headed thesis or hypothesis), points out why this idea is important, provides the line of argument, and specifies the content of the body of the paper/essay. The body uses the collected and analyzed evidence and logical reasoning to refute alternative arguments and to develop the main line of argument; that is, support the assertion and conclusion parts of the main argument. The body should have subheadings or sections discussing the various parts of the argument. The conclusion provides a brief fresh summary of the main argument and states the main decision that emerges from the argument, as well as introducing future research flowing from the argument. Citation is about giving credit to the sources of ideas and information you put in your paper/essay. If you borrowed ideas and information but you do not provide citations, you are guilty of a theft technically called plagiarism.

4. **Referencing or Citation Styles:**
   a) **Citation Styles:**
      ➤ **The American Psychological Association Style (APA):**
         - This is the standard system within the social sciences
         - In-text Reference: It requires that the last name of the author, the year of publication and the specific page number(s) (if a quotation) be enclosed in brackets within the body of the text. According to Adu-Febiri (2001, p. 5).
         - Title at the end of the essay/paper/report: "References"
         - Book: Single Author: Ofori, Everett. (2002). *Green Canadians: Dreams and fears.* Terrace: Kwame Publishing.
         - Book: Two Authors: Adu-Febiri, F. & Ofori, E. (2004). *Succeeding in Canadian Society.* Sooke: CCB Publishing.
         - Book: Three or More Authors: Adjibolosoo, S., Mensah, J. & Ofori-Amoah, B. (1999). *Making the Human Factor Work for Africa.* Tema: Accra Press.
         - Edited Book: Adu-Febiri, F. (ed.). (2000). *First Nations Students Talk Back.* Victoria: Camosun College Printing.
         - Journal Article: Adu-Febiri, F. (2006). "The Destiny of Cultural Diversity in a Globalized World". *Review of Human Factor Studies,* Vol. 12(1): 30-64.

      ➤ **The Modern Language Association Style (MLA):**
         - Like the APA style, it calls for the name of the author and the page number to be enclosed in brackets within the body of the text. However, unlike the APA, there is no requirement to include the year of publication.

   b) **Footnotes and Endnotes:**
      ➤ They are numbers, usually superscripts, that direct the reader to a full reference and/or comments.
         - Footnotes are consecutively numbered notes located at the bottom of a page.
         - Endnotes are consecutively numbered notes located at the end of the paper/essay.
         - Books and/or articles referred to in the footnotes/endnotes should be part of the reference/cited works/bibliography section.

An Example of a Term Paper:

The following article was first published as Adu-Febiri, F. (2002). Productive Diversity in the Classroom: Practising the Theories of Differences in Learning Styles. CDTL Brief, a publication of the Centre for Development of Teaching and Learning, National University of Singapore, Vol. 5. No. 6, pp. 3-5.

Practicing the Theories of Differences in Learning Styles in the Classroom

1. Introduction:

The classroom in many societies is a representation of people with different social class, gender, age, ability, ableness, sexuality, religious, racial, and/or ethnic backgrounds, as well as different personality types. Many of these differences are reflected in the multiplicity of learning styles of students. The irony is that most classrooms tend to cater mainly to the learning style needs of a particular group. According to Ginsburg (2001a, p. 109),

> Most university instruction is geared for abstract sequential learning. We emphasize the development of analytical skills and focus most classes on theoretical and conceptual issues; we eagerly give "corrective feedback" and often, if inadvertently, encourage perfectionism; we rely more on lectures than group discussions and in our small groups we feature the cut and thrust of debate over the exchange of feelings and spiritual insights.

The above observation of Jerry Ginsburg's seems very true even in most pre-university classrooms in many societies. So far, due to lack of recognition and facilitation of differences in learning styles, diversity in the classroom frustrates many students and teachers. The result is that development of fruitful learning and teaching is stunted. If the classroom is to motivate students to learn effectively, efficiently, and with joy rather than pain, the differences in their learning styles should be taken into account in the design and delivery of courses. To succeed in facilitating productive diversification in the classroom, the main principles of productive diversity—full inclusion and accommodation—must be diligently applied to course content, materials, assessment criteria, and delivery. Since the practice of these diversity principles is tedious, teachers must be convinced of diversity benefits first.

2. The Body:

Different Learning Styles

Scholars of learning and thinking have identified many learning styles (c.f. Jung 1971; Kolb 1976; Wheeler 1980; Butler 1984; Myers and McCaulley 1985; Gregorc 1985; Belensky *et al* 1986; Tobias 1990; and Gibbs 1992 for detailed discussion of learning styles). For analytical purposes, the learning styles identified in the literature can be integrated into what Gregorc (1985) designates as concrete sequential learning, abstract sequential learning, abstract random learning, and concrete random learning (Ginsburg 2001), and various combinations of these styles. The existence of diversity of learning styles has serious pedagogical implications. However, many classrooms ignore the implications of diversity of learning styles. The result is the prevalence of parochial approaches to learning in the education system (Rogers 2001) that homogenize the learning process of a diversity of students. This serves the interest of the status quo but kills initiative, innovation, and creativity that are needed to produce productive workers and citizens. Students and society benefit from productive diversity in the classroom, and adapting pedagogy to different learning styles promotes productive diversity.

Developing Diversity in Pedagogy

Although students have different learning styles, the conventional approach to learning presented to them in the school system makes them think that other pedagogies are either not right or are only useful outside the classroom. "Indeed, traditional schooling might have taught them [students] that…teachers are endowed with the information and that their role is to listen, take notes and be ready to reproduce the notes in the examination" (James 2001, p. 47). Because of this privileging of the conventional learning/teaching style, students are likely to initially resist the introduction of other pedagogies. For example, in a class where I use a delivery system that involves small-group discussions on the selected topic to identify problems with the text before I do a presentation on the topic, students initially complain that they expect to be lectured before group exercises. Many of the students come to like the approach later when they realize that it makes lecture presentations more meaningful. Introducing pedagogy that validates or legitimizes the neglected learning styles in the classroom will initially be resisted but will eventually flourish when the benefits of such diversity become evident. The bigger challenge, however, is how to successfully design and deliver curricula relevant to the multiplicity of learning styles represented in the classroom.

From the literature (Anderson 2001; Clarke 2001; Ginsburg 2001), it is clear that the main areas that require diversification are course content, material, assessment criteria, delivery, and accessibility. Below are some details of how I practice the principle of diversity in these areas in my classroom.

Content

In my courses I ensure that content covers a diversity of dimensions in the subject area: methodologies, methods, perspectives, theories/models, concepts, empirical evidence, and practices/applications.

Material

Particular attention is paid to the sources of reading materials for my classes. Inclusiveness is imperative in this process. Materials are selected from scholarly books, refereed journals, the Internet, magazines and newspapers, videos, documents, and statistical data produced from academic and non-academic perspectives with diversity of affiliations. For example, my "Legal and Political History of First Nations—White Relations in Canada" course uses texts written by Western academics, Aboriginal academics, and Aboriginal and Non-Aboriginal students.

Assessment Criteria

In the interest of diversity of learning styles, it is important that there are a variety of assessment components and options built into a course. My typical course has the following assessment criteria: Individual critical reviews, small-group discussions of selected chapters of texts to generate questions for class discussions, small-group discussions of term paper/research essay, class discussions, student oral presentations, research essay/term paper, multiple-choice mid-term exam, and essay-type final exam. In my Research Methods course, weekly laboratory sessions are an additional component. Bi-weekly workshops are an integral feature of my Workplace Diversity class. The grades are fairly distributed over the various assessment criteria. This minimizes the risk of experimenting with new learning styles for students.

Delivery

Like the assessment criteria, my course delivery takes learning style diversity into account. A combination of delivery modes is used in the same course. The instructor's interactive presentation in which students are motivated to make comments and ask and answer questions at any point, are combined with videos, skits, readings, labs, group/class discussions, and workshops. Transparencies, PowerPoint presentations, and the chalkboard are used as aids. All these delivery methods are well integrated into the main theme of the course.

Accessibility

A key principle of classroom diversity is flexibility of the teacher and the class organization. Flexibility entails the teacher being accessible to all students by providing diversity of avenues for interaction and participation. I have practised this flexibility in a number of ways: sometimes I leave the last five minutes of class time to meet with students who are not available during my regular office hours because of the demands of their family situation, job situation and/or other classes. I hold regular office hours at various times of day and days of the week, as well as make room for students to see me by appointment. Those students for whom none of the above options works can reach me through voice mail or email. With regard to accommodating students for participation, there have been instances where I have allowed students to bring their pre-school children to class.

Guidelines and Boundaries

The growing representation of diversity in the classroom heightens the emotional dimension of learning/teaching. To validate these emotions and channel them to facilitate learning/teaching in the classroom, the teacher and students must work together to develop clear guidelines and boundaries at the start of the class. The high points of these guidelines and boundaries should be respect, safety, support, sensitivity, and zero tolerance of abuse.

From the above discussion on attempts to create and implement diversity in pedagogy to reflect the variety of learning styles of students, it is clear that the process is complex and tedious. However, it is worthwhile pursuing it because it enhances student success by providing students from various backgrounds with voices in the classroom, encouraging student-teacher and student-student dialogue, and helping all students to identify with the learning process in the classroom. Not surprisingly, hardly do students fail or perform poorly in my courses in which diversity is conscientiously practised. An important thing that I have learned from the classroom diversity efforts is that to be successful, one has to possess both diversity competency (Cox and Beale 1997) and human factor competency (Adu-Febiri 2001), apart from motivation. Diversity competency is the ability to use awareness of differences, knowledge and understanding of differences, and facilitation skills to leverage differences to benefit people and organizations. Teachers need this competency in addition to the human factor competencies of commitment, dedication, loving-kindness, acceptance, persistence, responsibility and accountability to effectively facilitate productive diversity in the classroom. The school system should provide teachers with adequate incentives and support to acquire and apply the necessary competencies to make classroom diversity work.

3. **Conclusion:**

Diversity in learning styles exists in the classroom, and if not well facilitated, frustrates both learners and teachers. Despite this situation most classrooms continue to experience monolithic approaches to learning. It takes a lot of work to facilitate productive diversity in the classroom, but it is doable and is worth the effort. Diversity works in the classroom, and it works well when teachers value full inclusion, are motivated, supported, and provided with the necessary competencies. The growing diversity in the classroom represents learning style differences, and provides opportunities for teachers to substantially contribute to developing a productive labour force and productive citizens.

Writing Term Papers and Research Essays

As mentioned earlier, most literature on term papers and research essays focus on the "writing" aspect. They usually provide instructions or advice on writing. Chapter Six of Richard Floyd's (1995) book--*Success in the Social Sciences: Writing and Research for Canadian Students*-- on term papers and research essays is typical:

Writing Comfortably:

- Keep your expectations reasonable
- Use your own vocabulary; use thesaurus sparingly
- Use simple statements that express the intention of your points
- If you have access to a computer program with a grammar-checking feature, you should use it only to verify the correctness of what you have written
- Use formal language rather than slang
- Use jargon or concepts (discipline-specific language) that you can explain
- Surprise your reader from time to time by using some jokes once a while
- Be yourself: do not try to sound like someone else or copy another writer's style in your work
- Read what you put on the page as you write in order to maintain a consistent voice

Writing Clearly:

- Try to avoid jargon, but when it is necessary interpret it clearly to the reader/marker

- Impress your marker with data and argument rather than high-sounding words and grammar
- Combine a variety of short, medium, and longer sentences
- Deal with the main idea and each of the supporting ideas separately: present one idea at a time
- Each paragraph should have one idea: it should introduce, discuss, and summarize the idea

Editing:

➤ Make up your mind to write more than one draft of your paper/essay: no paper/essay is letter-perfect the first time through.
  - While you are writing the first version, your energies should be focused on getting your ideas in the right order instead of refinement

Creating Headings and Subheadings:

➤ These are ready, easy reference points that break your paper into logical sections to help the reader/marker follow the progress of your paper/essay.
  - Each of the headings and subheadings should be necessary, and placed at a transition point
  - Use the right number: not too many / not too few
  - Keep them short and informative
  - Make them interesting or catchy

Creating Introductions and Conclusions:

- Set out your own line of analysis, comparison, and/or evaluation of the idea you are writing about in your introduction to provide context for your paper/essay.
- Your conclusion should show that you have achieved what you have set out to do in your introduction; you can also talk about the implication of your findings, and comment on the limitations of your paper/essay.

Choosing Referencing or Citation Style:

➤ Every piece of information you include in your paper/essay (a quote, a fact, statistics, or paraphrase) must be referenced; that is, give credit to the original author.

- Whenever you quote one or two lines enclose them in quotation marks and add the author, year of publication and page number in brackets
- Whenever you quote three or more lines, indent and add author, year of publication and page number in brackets
- If the quotation extends onto more than one page in your source, use a slash mark to indicate the page break
- Whenever you use paraphrased material from your notes, add the author, year of publication and page number in brackets
- When you revise your draft, put the bracketed references in the appropriate citation format. Since there are so many styles, the best strategy is to ask your professor for her/his preference

Revise Your Draft:

- ➤ Revise Middle Paragraphs
  - Check topic sentences
  - Integrate research material by linking the topic sentences with research details, analysis, interpretation argument and explanation
- ➤ Revise the thesis and essay structure
- ➤ Revise the introduction
- ➤ Revise the conclusion

Edit the Entire Paper/Essay:

- ➤ **Check Tone**
  - Word choice
  - Appropriate pronouns: First-person, Second-person, Third-Person

- ➤ **Check Sentence Structure**
  - Clauses and phrases

- ➤ **Check for sentence effectiveness**
  - Sentence length, pattern, variations, hooks,
  - Transition words and phrases

- ➤ **Check Verbs**
  - Main and auxiliary verbs
  - Verb tenses
  - Active and passive voices
  - Subject-verb agreement

- ➢ **Check Pronouns:**
  - Possessive pronouns
  - Subject and object pronouns

- ➢ **Check Punctuation**
  - Comma
  - Semicolon
  - Colon
  - Dash
  - Parentheses and brackets
  - Italics
  - Apostrophe
  - Hyphen

- ➢ **Check Quotations**
  - When to quote and not to quote
  - Using quotation effectively
  - Indicating changes in quotation
  - Quotation format
  - What to acknowledge
  - Systems of reference
    - APA System
    - MLA System
    - ASA System

- ➢ **Proofread**
  - Abbreviations
  - Capitalization
  - Numbers
  - Spelling
  - Omissions
  - Inconsistencies in argument

Conclusion

Producing term papers and research essays is surely challenging. However, it could be exciting rather than daunting if you are knowledgeable about originality, creativity, appropriate structure and content, solid evidence, systematic reasoning, and writing. Spend time and effort to acquire this knowledge.

Chapter Twenty-Four

Writing Excellent Reports

Like essays, report writing is an important component of many courses in the post-secondary education system. Depending upon your major, you will be doing more of one type of report than others. Whereas in the social sciences book reports are more popular, laboratory or research reports and business reports are predominant in the physical sciences and business administration programs respectively. Whether you are writing an essay, book report, lab report, or business report, there are certain fundamental things you need to consider. Your writing should be clear, concise, and forceful (Northey and Tepperman 1993). Beyond these similarities, there are unique requirements for each report type. Book reports focus on summary and/or assessment of content and publication details, lab reports put more emphasis on objectivity and procedures, and business reports highlight presentation and recommendations.

Book Reports

There are three major variations of book reports: informative book report, analytic book report, and literary book report (Northey and Tepperman 1993). The common thread connecting these three book report types is that they all provide a brief, coherent summary of the book. What differentiates them is the focus of the report. An informative book report limits itself to a concise and systematic summary, but an analytic book report and a literary book report go beyond summarizing. While in addition to a summary, an analytic book report concentrates on assessing the strengths and weaknesses of the whole book, a literary book report allows the reviewer the freedom to do an in-depth discussion of any aspect or feature of interest to him/her (Northey 1993). Since social science instructors rarely make their students write informative book reports and literary reviews, it is more important to focus on how to write an analytic book report than the other two types of book report.

How to Write an Analytic Book Report or Book Review

- Start by providing detailed bibliographical information about the book: "Author's Name, Full Title (plus subtitle if present), Editor (when present), Edition (if any), the Place, Publisher and Date of Publication, and the Number of Pages" (O'Day 1991, p. 104).
- Indicate the book's subject, focus, and purpose.

- Outline the organizational features of the book: Chapters, sections, and special features such as appendices, notes, and indexes.
- Highlight the main theme and thesis of the book.
- Show how the author argues out the main thesis.
- Comment on the kind of data used.
- Point out the strengths and weaknesses in the areas of assumption, order of presentation, logical flow of the argument, key evidence, contradictions, biases, accomplishment of objectives, and style, supporting them with examples and quotes from the book.
- Draw conclusions: succinct summary, special meaning, impact, a new insight.

Example of a Book Report:

The following book review report was written by Francis Adu-Febiri and was first published in 2000 in the Review of Human Factor Studies, Vol. 6(1): 132-135.

Adjibolosoo, S. (ed.), 2000. The Human Factor in Shaping the Course of History and Development. Lanham: University of America, Inc. 313p. ISBN 0-7618-1613-5.

It is apparent, and most people believe, that what shapes the course of history and development is technology. The Industrial Revolution transformed human society and the Information Revolution is fast changing the world. It is in this light that this book goes against the grain of conventional wisdom. This book, comprised of twelve chapters contributed by fourteen highly educated intellectuals, proposes that it is people rather than technology that make things happen. This idea was planted in the mind of the editor when he was a child by his grandfather in a fishing village in southern Ghana during one of their fishing expeditions. In response to the editor's question, "Where have all the fishes gone?" the grandfather said, "People have caught them all..." (emphasis supplied). Extending this idea to the larger human society, the book emphasizes that:

The course of human history and development on planet earth has been shaped by various categories of people using their acquired HF characteristics. Human history is replete with a gamut of examples relating to the actions of men and women who have contributed either to the progress or underdevelopment of their nations... Democracy, authoritarianism, dictatorship, apartheid, Nazism, capitalism, socialism, communism, and many others like these are human creations. The extent to which any of these ideologies contributes positively or negatively to development programs, industrial progress, and social welfare is determined by the state of the HF traits of the individuals involved (p. 4).

Chapter six captures this fulcrum of the book when it states that "positive HF attributes are the key to improving human welfare, and that the ultimate resource of any country is its people, its human ingenuity and HF attributes" (p. 129). Focusing on the transfer of marketing technology, chapter eight provides a powerful illustration of the thesis that people rather than technology make things happen. It argues that:

The inability of developing economies to effectively create, acquire, adapt, utilize or maintain imported marketing technology is not only a result of experts' a priori assumptions regarding the technology and the recipient country, as exemplified by Levitt (1983) and Kindra (1984 p. ix), but are also inherent in the neglect of a variety of cultural and human dimensions collectively referred to as the HF (p. 166).

In essence the success of any invention and/or transfer of technology essentially depends on the level of human qualities in the people involved. Societies that focus on technological development without paying enough attention to continuously improving the human quality of their people will always experience growing human poverty, high inequalities, and low quality of life.

The human qualities the book discusses include knowledge, skills, and traits such as social relations, values, morals, aesthetics, abilities, and potentials. Chapter three uses the concept of social capital to discuss the dynamics that induce the human qualities of trust and trustworthiness emphasizing the relationships among personalized social relations, culture, the level of human factor development, and trust. It is postulated that elaborate social capital, that is, personalized social networks, reflects and causes human factor decay and/or underdevelopment. In fact, the underlying force of polarized racial, ethnic, political, religious, income, and gender inequalities may be elaborate social capital formation which is an indicator of HF decay. Thus the development of appropriate HF traits can save on resources otherwise used to form social capital and manage conflicts inequalities generate. In effect, the stronger the HF, the higher the level of trust and stronger the performance of the economy. This is because "higher levels of trust might actually require less investment in social capital and can therefore set free resources for productive activities that were previously employed in the formation of social capital" (p. 35). Japan's economic miracle and other economic miracles of the world are the result of focus on developing the appropriate HF characteristics and trust based on personalized networks (i.e., social capital).

Human history and social development are replete with collective problems that require collective actions to resolve. This is the theme of chapter four. It proposes a meta-theoretical situational modeling that incorporates appropriate HF to deal with the collective decision-making dilemmas that face humanity. Specifically it theorizes that these dilemmas can be resolved through education and training programs of principle-based decision-making that emphasize human qualities of tolerance, integrity, non-violence, creative appreciation of the natural environment, responsibility to one's community, and commitment to the global human community.

Without knowing the beliefs and values of a people you cannot really understand their attitudes, behaviours and actions. Chapters nine and twelve provide detailed analysis of the relationships between religious values and the realization of human potentialities. Fatalistic Islamic religious values predominant in Indonesian Muslims lead to HF decay and/or underdevelopment (p. 212), and thus tend to arrest the socioeconomic development of this resource-rich country. Likewise, Christian fundamentalism in Alabama might stifle "the development of badly needed new science curricula, textbooks and methodologies" needed for "the development of curious, logical, intellectual, and imaginative tendencies in students and by so doing, decreasing the interest of students in and about the fields of science and technology" (p. 300). To rectify these situations, it is intimated, these religious beliefs should be replaced by value systems such as "communications theology" that will motivate people to develop HF characteristics to (a) "keep a balance between a ritual-oriented life and material-oriented one, enabling them to perform their tasks as vicegerents of this world" (p. 212) and (b) "learn to think for themselves and not depend only on revealed, untested knowledge... " (p. 306).

Unlike the above discussion of religion as an HF decay agency, chapter seven highlights the positive role the world's religions can play in halting the existing ecological crisis and promoting global sustainable development. These world spiritual traditions are very useful in the quest for environmental stewardship because they embody HF traits that can create appropriate awareness that "the abuse and exploitation of nature for immediate gain is unjust, immoral, and unethical" (p. 144). From the injunctions and exhortations of Judaism, Islam, Christianity, Hinduism, Buddhism, and other spiritual traditions appropriate human qualities can be honed to develop and implement a code for environmentally sound and sustainable development.

Chapters ten and eleven carry the discussion of the cultural dimension of the HF into the controversial realms of language empowerment and English language export service. They clearly articulated that "HF development is made more feasible through effective and appropriate modes of human communication—the primary one being language, which in modern times requires functional literacy" (p. 249). In other words, appropriate language is necessary to foster the HF, that is, our social, human, spiritual, moral, and aesthetic capital, as well as our individual abilities and potential.

Chapter ten portrays language as a resource that guarantees the 'appropriation' of knowledge. As such its universal promotion and development will benefit humanity by causing equality, fairness, and productivity on both the national and global scale. For example, colonial English, turned official and national language in many African countries, is a resource with immense potential; those who know its value have cultivated it carefully so as to reap the benefits of social, economic, and political knowledge associated with functional proficiency in it (p. 246).

It is in this light that many countries of the world are importing the services of English language teachers that chapter eleven discusses so insightfully. English language teaching service can be "a beneficial civilizing act" for it may "enhance communication, understanding, and goodwill" that will enable "diverse peoples to live together peacefully and with mutual respect" (pp. 279 and 280). The fact is, the exported English language teacher can contribute to the promotion of the universal, fundamental human qualities of social harmony and cooperation, hard work and duty to society, moral responsibility and accountability, etc., in the English language classroom anywhere in the world. In essence, the author of this chapter, is correct when he concludes that:

> There can be no such place as a classroom in which values are not exchanged and principles of behaviour not explored. In accordance with the expectations of my employers, I teach the English that the present global community accepts for its standard. I also do my best to attend to the needs of my students to develop those human factor qualities in themselves that will make their lives more completely satisfying to them. I make no apologies for this. It is my responsibility as a teacher (p. 282).

The power of the English language is real power, for it is "on course to becoming universal on this planet" (p. 280), but so far it is the elite who usually benefit from the exported English language service. Herein lies the emphasis of chapter ten that the masses need to harness the power of language "in order to make sense of other essential HF traits" (p. 251). The masses of the world "are already intelligent and full of savvy and wisdom... but to become a functional part of our new global village they need to be rid of ignorance by empowering them through a comprehensive HF functional literacy" (p. 251).

This empowerment of the masses will happen only when societal and organizational leaders are committed to it. The type of leadership that will initiate and/or genuinely implement HF development programs and projects is the leadership that has human factor competence. That is, leaders who possess the ability and commitment to serve others with integrity and humility. Such leaders, according to authors of chapter five, are servant-leaders in contrast to command-leaders. The chapter succinctly points out that "Highly motivated and well-trained human resources provide the only assurance that any organization will be effective in accomplishing its goals. Servant-leaders motivate followers through investing in them and empowering them to do their best" (p. 71).

The challenge is how to produce servant-leaders. In the view of this chapter, "with encouragement, training, and means of measuring leadership development, more servant-leaders will emerge" (p. 97). However, it does not provide a program for encouraging and training these leaders. In fact, it is evident throughout the book that there is an urgent need for comprehensive HF education and training to equip societal leaders and masses to positively shape the course of history and development. Unfortunately, however, though the book scores very high on analytical prognoses and theoretical prescriptions, it does not describe in detail practical programs and projects that could be used to develop the appropriate human factor characteristics.

In spite of the above weakness, the book makes a significant contribution to the development literature by drawing attention to a neglected lynch pin of human history and development, the HF characteristics of people. It surely serves as a challenge to intellectuals, politicians, and development gurus to provide ideas, support and funding to create practical, feasible HF education and training programs to produce HF competent people who will positively shape the course of human society. I will strongly recommend it to students, teachers, researchers, and practitioners of development.

Research or Laboratory Report

The physical sciences and some social science courses such as research methods that involve laboratory sections require that students produce lab or research reports. Lab reports are designed to concisely and objectively communicate research hypothesis, data collections procedures, data analysis, results, and interpretation within a scientifically acceptable format (O'Day 1991, p. 110). Before writing and formatting the research report, plan it by considering factors such as:

- The readers of the report (specialists or non-specialists).
- The appropriate style of presentation (active or passive voice).
- The appropriate style of documentation (referencing).
- The space allocated to each section of the report.
- The appropriate length of the report.

With respect to formatting, the literature on research report writing tends to agree on the following broad format (O'Day 1991, Northey and Tepperman 1993):

- Title or cover page
- Abstract or executive summary

- Introduction
- Materials and methods
- Results or findings
- Discussion or interpretation
- Conclusion
- References
- Appendices

Title:
- Should be catchy.
- Must provide enough information to give the reader a sense of the general and specific issues of the research.
- The title page should include, in addition to the title, your name and other relevant information, e.g., the number of the course and professor's name.

Abstract:
- Provide a concise summary of the objectives, methods, findings, and conclusions in two hundred words or less. If executive summary option is selected, add a summarized version of recommendations.

Introduction and Literature Review:
- Clearly state the aim, issue, and/or hypothesis.
- Place the research in the context of other research and ideas.
- Point out any ethical issues that arose and explain how they were resolved.

Research Design and Materials:
- List the materials and equipment used in the study.
- State the design selected and explain why it was selected.
- Discuss the various steps you went through in collecting the data.

Quantitative Study:
- Explain how the variables were measured.
- Describe the population and type of sample.
- Explain how the sample was selected.

Qualitative Study:
- Explain how you gained access to the information/data.
- Point out the factors that influenced the selection of the individuals, groups, documents, events, etc., that were studied.

Data Analysis:
- This is the heart of the report and a section of most interest to specialists.
- It begins with a clear statement of the main findings followed by quantitative data and/or verbal description of the main and secondary findings.
- The length should be at least one-third of the report.

Quantitative Data:
- Label tables, graphs and statistics, put them in appropriate format, and discuss them in the text.
- Provide appropriate statistical analysis.
- Provide technical interpretation of the findings.

Qualitative Data:
- Tables and graphs (if included) should be properly labelled and discussed in the text.
- Describe the social and cultural context of the data.
- Do not identify the places and people you describe in your study.

Discussion:
- ➢ Interpret the findings and critically examine their significance in light of the research question or hypothesis.
  - How reliable is the data?
  - To what extent do the findings relate to the study's objectives and other studies on the topic?
  - What explains the findings?
  - What does the pattern revealed by the data mean?

Conclusion:
- Highlight the main findings.
- Indicate the strengths and weaknesses of the research.
- Draw out the practical implications.
- Discuss the implications for future research.

References and Citations:
- Use a proper and consistent form of documenting sources.
- Place the reference section immediately after the text.
- List the sources in the reference section in alphabetical order according to author's last name.
- Provide complete bibliographical citations of the sources cited in the report.

Appendix:
- Put tables, summaries of raw data, questionnaire, etc., that would interrupt the flow of the report if incorporated into the analysis section here.
- Refer to them in the analysis section.

Business Report

Business reports are written to provide information and/or make recommendations with respect to production, sales, project progress, course of action, and/or a particular business problem. The effectiveness of a business report depends on where the essence of the report is placed, organization of information, the tone, level of conciseness, accuracy, objectivity, and visual appeal (Northey and Tepperman 1993).

The Essence of the Report:
- Provide the essence of the report in the form of main findings and recommendations as an executive summary.

Organization of Information:
- Provide sections detailing the purpose, method, findings, recommendations, and conclusions.
- Provide a title page, table of contents, appendix, bibliography, and letter of transmittal (a memo introducing the report to the reader placed after the title page.

Tone:
- Be formal.

Level of Conciseness:
- Make the report brief and to the point.

Accuracy:
- Ensure that information in the report is factual.

Objectivity:
- Prevent personal biases from creeping into the report.

Visual Attractiveness:
- Use title page, tables, charts, fonts, bullets, and/or pictures to create visual appeal.

CHAPTER TWENTY-FIVE

EXCELLING IN TESTS AND EXAMINATIONS

Introduction

Many students are scared of tests and examinations. "Imagine how fun courses would be if there were no tests and examinations," a student once said. Tests and examinations would not take the fun out of courses if there is no social pressure to succeed, students are certain that the exam questions will focus on the material they have studied well, and students have the skills to answer exam questions effectively. The point is that students think that what makes tests and examinations scary is the pressure or high expectations from peers, family members, and teachers. However, the real problem is that many students just do not have the required skills to take tests and examinations. The fact is, in a culture where failure or losing is shameful and tests/exams measure success, exams will always be scary. Having the requisite test and examination skills would very much reduce the scariness. While the fear of exams, what some students refer to as "exam fever," cannot be completely overcome, students can develop strategies to avoid going blank and do well in examinations. The most useful strategies are a) to thoroughly know and understand the course material, and the commonly used terms and concepts in examination questions and b) acquire the necessary examination skills.

Exams: What Are They About?

As O'Day (1991, p. 75) powerfully puts it, an important aspect of all test/examination methods is that they test your ability

- To read.
- To recall.
- To think.
- To communicate what you are thinking.

You will not only be asked to reproduce memorized information, but also to use it in new ways (O'Day 1991). You will have to analyze, discuss, define, outline, apply, review, explain, compare and contrast information. To do this you will have to know the information and understand it very well. In good courses a diverse number of testing questions and formats are used to test students' level of knowledge and understanding of certain main concepts, perspectives, applications, and their relationships.

Authors such as Giarrusso *et al* (2001), Northey & Tepperman (1993), Floyd (1995) and O'Day (1991) who write about examination taking skills and techniques have identified the following:

Examination Types:

In general there are two major types of examinations:
- Objective type
- Essay type

Objective Examinations:

Objective examinations involve short answers. They are usually made up of:
- True or False questions
- Multiple Choice questions
- Fill-in-the-Blank and Matching questions
- Short Answer questions

The biggest difficulty with objective questions is that they are hardly clear and precise. They therefore require very careful reading and analysis before an answer is attempted.

True or False Questions: Ask whether a statement or claim is true or false. In this type of exam qualifiers or key words such as ALL, MOST, FEW, NONE, USUALLY, RARELY, NEVER, MORE, EQUAL, LESS, GOOD, and BAD suggest that the statement is false.

Example: The true-false statements: "All Asians are Mathematics whizzes." FALSE. "Some Asians are Mathematics whizzes." TRUE.

Multiple Choice: The question is asked followed by a series of answers from which you will have to select the best or most correct one(s).

Example: Many international students experience confusion and discomfort when they first come to Canada. What is the correct term for this experience?

a) Ethnocentrism
b) Identity Crisis
c) Flu
d) Culture Shock
e) Accident

Processes of answering the above multiple choice question correctly:

- Read and analyze the question very carefully and come up with an answer before reading the multiple-choice answers. Look at the answer choices. If your answer is found among the possible answers it is likely that your answer is correct.
- If on the other hand your answer is not one of the possible answers, eliminate all obviously incorrect answers. The remaining is likely to be a correct answer.
- If after crossing out all the obvious incorrect answers you still have two or three possible answers remaining, make an educated guess if the exam instruction does not say that you lose marks by guessing incorrectly.

Fill-in-the-Blank Questions: You are asked to add a specific word or phrase to complete a statement.

- Make sure that when you add the word/phrase the statement makes complete sense and reads properly.

Example: North America is made up of three countries, namely, Canada, _____ and Mexico.

Matching Key Words/Phrases:

- Match up the ones that you are positive about first.
- As you eliminate the ones you are sure about, your final pairings will become easier through this process of elimination.

Example: Duck   Mary
         Pancake   Water
         Sarah   Pencil
         Pen   Bread
         Rain   Sparrow

Short Answer: You are usually asked to provide no longer than a two-sentence definition of a concept or terminology.

- Therefore memorize the definitions of all major concepts in the course.
- Provide an example after the definition.

Example: What is sustainability?

It is meeting the needs of the present generation without destroying the ability of future generations to meet their needs. For example, cutting timber for the present generation's use and planting trees for the use of future generations.

Essay Examinations

Essay examination is the type that presents the most difficulty for many students. In this format the student is expected to provide an academic, coherent and comprehensive answer in essay form to a teacher-produced question. In the words of O'Day (1991, p. 75) you are asked "to put meaningful sentences into paragraphs and organize those paragraphs into intellectual composition." Specifically, you may be requested to simply:

- Describe: Give an answer to a "HOW" and/or "WHAT" question.
- Compare: Show similarities and differences and draw a meaningful conclusion.
- Discuss: Debate; provide your interpretation and insight.
- Analyze: Classify or categorize into elements and highlight their relationships and patterns.
- Account: Provide facts about.
- Outline: State the main points without developing them in detail.
- Examine: Inspect carefully, inquire into, or investigate.
- Explain: Make plain, provide an answer to "WHY" and "HOW" questions.
- Review or evaluate: Highlight the main theme, discuss the main strengths and weaknesses, and provide suggestions by addressing the weaknesses.

O'Day (1991, p. 81) hits the nail on the head when he points out that writing an essay examination is like writing a research essay or term paper. The only difference is that you usually have to produce an answer to the question solely from memory. Thus you cannot go out and research the topic while the exam is underway. However, like any essay, follow the valuable advice of Northey & Tepperman (1986) and O'Day (1991) that you should:

- Read through the questions.
- Make sure you understand what is asked.
- Choose your questions and re-read them very carefully.
- Divide your time equally amongst the different questions.
- Plan a method of attacking the problem.
- Write an outline that is relevant and logical.
- Write an answer as neatly or legibly as possible.
- Re-read your answer and make corrections.

Many students' answers to essay exams do not:
- Answer every part of the question.
- Respond directly to the main focus of the question.
- Provide introduction and conclusion.
- Provide illustrative examples.

Yet answering all parts of the exam question, focusing on the main issue of the question, providing examples to support the claims made, and providing a clear introduction and insightful conclusion are the fundamental requirements of essay exams.

Example: Below is a student's answer (to an essay exam question in a third year university class) that has the above problems.

Question: What are the disadvantages of Capitalism?

Student's Answer: Capitalism has been criticized for being unstable, distributing income unevenly, and not adequately reflecting social objectives.

Capitalism is criticized for being unstable because it is a system that is regulated by the business cycle. Critics maintain that any system that is based on the business cycle is inherently unstable. In times of economic boom there is high employment, but in times of economic bust there is high unemployment. Therefore in a capitalist system high levels of unemployment is a common occurrence.

Income is distributed unevenly in a market capitalist society. The capitalist accumulates vast amounts of wealth, while the workers are paid low wages. There are no forms of income redistribution to supplement low wages of workers since government intervention in the economy is undesirable. The workers' pay does not accurately reflect the value of their labour.

Capitalism has also been criticized for not adequately reflecting social objectives, and it doesn't. Since there is no government intervention in the economy there are no social services such as unemployment insurance or universal healthcare. Those who can't afford healthcare or lose their jobs must fend for themselves. There is no social safety net. Most people in society value social safety nets and welcome government intervention in such areas. The objective of market capitalism is profit maximization so social objectives are ignored.

Course Instructor's Comment: Thoughtful discussion of issues covered, but several issues omitted. Based on the comment she gave the student a B-.

Issues Student Neglected:
- Anarchy of markets
- Environmental Damage
- No income for those who don't work
- Monopoly Profits: no incentives for innovations; high prices
- Absence of complete information for rational decision

Other weaknesses:
- Incomplete introduction: doesn't mention the advantages of capitalism
- No suggestions to minimize disadvantages of capitalism
- No illustrative examples
- No conclusion

Open Book and Take-Home Exams

To avoid plagiarism and time wasting (Northey and Tepperman 1993):

- Study the course material thoroughly before the exam.
- Aim at producing critical analysis and providing concrete illustrative examples.
- Use books and/or notes only for specific facts and exact definitions of concepts you do not remember.

Test and Examination Tips

Many writers on this subject, particularly Northey and Tepperman (1993), O'Day (1991) and Giarrusso *et al* (2001) believe that the following tips work for many students taking exams:

Before the test/exam:
- Use old exams as a source of typical questions to guide your preparation.

- Review your material the night before the exam.
- Focus on understanding, not memorization.
- Get a good night's sleep.
- Get up at least several hours before the exam begins, and again, read some or all of your notes over.
- Do this preparation in a quiet place; do it alone.
- You should not arrive early for the examination; arrive just in time to enter the exam room and take your seat.

At the beginning of the exam:
- Be sure to listen carefully to any verbal instructions that are given by the teacher or whoever is administering the exam.
- Ask questions if the information is not clear.
- Read the complete exam before you start to write.
- Budget your time properly.
- Write your name and student number.

Writing the exam:
- Begin with the easy questions first and then progress to the more difficult.
- Write one continuous answer then move on to the next. If you have an idea for one question as you are writing another, make a note in the margin of the other question to remind yourself. Then get back to the question at hand.
- Understand what is being asked before you begin writing: underline key words and phrases in the question; think about what is being asked, make notes and then write.
- When you finish writing your examination re-read your answers to make necessary corrections.

CHAPTER TWENTY-SIX

CONCLUSION:
CONNECTED BUT NOT ASSIMILATED

Introduction

Many Canadian minorities desire to be full participants in Canadian society and academia without being culturally assimilated into the mainstream. This minority quest has contributed to the establishment of Canada's multiculturalism and employment equity policies. Canada's commitment to such cultural and educational inclusiveness has much to recommend it; the country has come a long way since the days when differences were punished (Fleras and Elliott 2002). Unfortunately, however, this multicultural commitment is not easily translated into practice that would fundamentally transform Canada's monoculturalism. The content, instruction methods, language, evaluation and other practices of the education system continue to promote and facilitate assimilation. "All this should warn us not to expect too much of multicultural education" (Fleras and Elliott 2002, p. 203).

Facts such as this and experiences of Canadian minorities suggest that Canadian society and education have not fundamentally adapted, and are not likely to adapt, to the diversity needs of minorities, at least in the near future. Therefore if new immigrants, refugees and international students want to succeed in Canada they need to adapt to the mainstream Canadian society. Hence the approach taken by this book is that to become successful in Canadian society, it entails adapting to the standard norms, dress codes, languages, communication styles, interaction patterns, technologies, expectations and practices of the mainstream monoculture. Is such adaptation assimilation? This book proposes that this adaptation process of minorities is integration, and will move to assimilation only when the minorities compromise their values and beliefs in the integration process. Put differently, integrating without assimilating is the key to minority success in Canadian society and its education system. Is it possible, feasible and practicable to integrate without assimilating? The content of this book highlights the conditions and strategies that facilitate the successful adaptation of new immigrants, refugees and international students to mainstream Canadian society and its education system without becoming assimilated.

Assimilation

At the core, assimilation is about cultural minorities internalizing the values and beliefs of the mainstream society and simultaneously losing or discarding their original values and beliefs. This process could be voluntary or involuntary. It is voluntary when minorities decide to jettison their own cultural values and beliefs and replace them with that of the dominant group without any direct force from social institutions, particularly the state, education system, religious organizations, and the family. Assimilation is involuntary when the state, religion, education and other social institutions force cultural minorities to adopt and practice mainstream values, beliefs and identities; official policies and practices of the Canadian state and religious institutions in the past moved minorities towards this path. A classic case is the experiences of the First Nations. Various pieces of legislation and the residential school system forced Aboriginal Canadians to abandon their indigenous values and beliefs for Euro-Canadian values and Christian beliefs (Adu-Febiri 2004). However since the 1970s, such policies and practices have been outlawed through the establishment of the 1971 Multiculturalism Policy and the enactment of the 1988 Multiculturalism Act. Yes, Euro-Canadian absorptive cultural involvement and exposure continue to pressure minorities to assimilate (Fleras and Elliott 2002), but it is slightly easier for minorities to resist such pressures because there are no legal and political forces to mitigate their resistance. Multiculturalism education and anti-racism education are constructed to further ease this pressure on cultural minorities in Canada to assimilate.

Multiculturalism Education and Anti-Racism Education

The declared goal of official multiculturalism in Canada is to completely eliminate cultural, political, social, and economic disadvantages against cultural and racial minorities. Multiculturalism education and anti-racism education are designed to implement this noble goal by systematically centering diversity in educational policies, programs, practices, and environments (Fleras and Elliott 2002). In short, multiculturalism education is to advance minority inclusiveness in the education system by exposing students from both minority and majority cultures to motivate them to inculcate and practice cultural diversity.

Anti-racism education, unlike multiculturalism education, focuses more on uprooting racism than changing the culture of schools. It "sets out to transform those aspects of education that exclude minority women and men, intentionally or not. In particular, it contests the power structures—institutional policies, practices, and procedures—that sustain racism" (Fleras and Elliott 2002, p. 210). It identifies and proposes strategies to eliminate racial biases "in mission statements, in cultures and subcultures, in power and decision-making arrangements, in rules, roles and relation-ships, and in how assets (both financial and human) are distributed" (Fleras and Elliott 2002, p. 211). In other words, anti-racism education aims at eliminating the roots of racism and racial discrimination rather than fostering cultural differences and dealing with prejudice and stereotypes.

These educational innovations and official multiculturalism are yet to achieve their objectives of making Canadian society and education inclusive. Until inclusiveness becomes a reality, new immigrants, refugees, international students, and cultural minorities in Canada should aim at integrating into the mainstream for the purposes of conventional material and social rewards as well as leverage and empowerment to push for further minority inclusion.

Integration

Productive integration is about cultural minorities adapting to the expectations, standards, and practices of the mainstream and being accepted by the dominant group without the minorities sacrificing their original cultural values, beliefs and identities. However, some race and ethnic relations scholars believe that cultural integration is more nominal than real (Fleras and Elliott 2002). What this belief does not take into account is the Canadian state's granting of formal equality to minorities and the successful adaptation of many minorities into the Canadian mainstream in spite of systemic barriers. The process of real integration of minorities into the Canadian mainstream began in the 1970s when they were granted formal legal equality. This formal equality satisfies the acceptance condition of cultural integration. With formal equality in place, minorities have the opportunity to adapt to the mainstream without being absorbed by it or assimilating. Some minorities have responded to this opportunity by constructing bifurcated or double lives for themselves. Individuals from many racial/ethnic minority and First Nations groups in Canada live successful double or multiple lives. They master and practice Euro-Canadian cultural knowledge, skills, expectations and standards of Canadian mainstream institutions and at the same time live according to their own ethnic values, beliefs and identities expected within their families and communities. It is these integration success stories of Canadian racial and ethnic minorities that have inspired the writing of this book to help guide new immigrants, refugees and international students to repeat, and to even surpass, these success stories.

Conclusion

Given the predominantly monocultural and monostructural realities of major Canadian social institutions, new immigrants, refugees and international students can be successful mainly by integrating into mainstream Canadian society and its education system from the margins. That is, true success of the racial and cultural minorities occurs when they connect with but not assimilate into the mainstream institutions, organizations and ideologies. Integration is feasible through mastering and utilizing the strategic resources such as appropriate knowledge and relevant skills, mentoring, networking, family and community support. These strategic resources are what would help racial and cultural minorities to open up the cracks in the Canadian inequality structure to obtain good jobs, become gainfully self-employed, excel in the education system, and live fulfilling lives.

BIBLIOGRAPHY

Abley, Mark. Sep 21, 2002. "A public humiliation: Somen Chowdury is a prize immigrant. He's lived in Quebec for 20 years. But thugs told him to 'go back where you came from'. *The Gazette*, D.1.

Adu-Febiri, Francis. 2001. "Human Factor Competency and the Performance Effectiveness of Hospitality Industry Professionals". In Senyo Adjibolosoo (Ed.). *Portraits of Human Behavior and Performance: The Human Factor in Action.* Lanham: University Press of America.

Adu-Febiri, Francis. 2003/04. "Facilitating Cultural Diversity in a Monolithic Global Economy: The Role of Human Factor Education." *International Journal of the Humanities*, Volume 1, 2003/04, pp. 885-908.

Adu-Febiri, Francis. 2004. *First Nations Students Talk Back: Voices of a Learning People*. Victoria, B.C.: Camosun College.

Anderson, Rae. 2001. "Empowering Students Through Feminist Pedagogy?". In Janice Newton *et al* (Eds*). Voices from the Classroom: Reflections on Teaching and Learning in Higher Education.* Aurora, Ontario: Garamond Press.

Ashante, Infantry. July 3, 1999. Echoes of bigotry; You don't have to be black to suffer prejudice: You just have to sound black, *Toronto Star*, A.1.

Barahona, Federico. April 2001. "Invisible: Diversity in Canadian Newsrooms." In *UBC Journalism Review Thunderbird Online Magazine*. Volume iii, Issue iv.

Beauchesne, Eric. Jan 27, 2004. Body language tells a lot at job interviews. *The Vancouver Sun*, F.1.

Belensky, M.F. *et al.* 1986. *Women's Ways of Knowing: The Development of Self, Voice, and Mind.* New York: Basic Books.

Benimadhu, Prem. Spring 1995. Adding value through diversity. *Canadian Business Review,* 22(1), 6.

Bethune, Brian. 7/1/2003. Austin Clarke. *Maclean's*, 116.26/27, 32.

Bohn, Glenn. May 19, 2001. Convicted officer gets probation; RCMP constable also faces gun restrictions for pointing weapon at a dentist's head. *The Vancouver Sun*, B.1.

Bourrie, Mark. March 1, 2000. Former Refugee Crashes "Old" Boys' Club. InterPress Service English News Wire.

Brown, David. Dec. 17, 2001. Marathon discrimination case ends. *Canadian HR Reporter*, 14.22, 1.

Butler, Kathleen. 1984. *Learning and Teaching Style: In Theory and Practice*. Columbia, CT: Learner's Dimension.

Chinese Businesswoman Finds Freedom and Success in Vancouver's Rubbish Starting with a lot of gumption; Emily Leung, an immigrant from Hong Kong, has built a multimillion-dollar recycling empire in Canada. Nov 21, 1994. *Christian Science Monitor*.

Choudry, Sujit. Nov. 25, 2002. Laws needed to ban racial profiling: 'For persons profiled, the indignity is real.' www.thestar.com (14/9/2004).

Chugani, Michael. Mar 9, 1998. 'Little Hong Kong' built by arrivals in Canada. *Hong Kong Standard* http://www.infoweb.newsbank.com...(14/9/2004).

Cialdini, Robert B. 1993. *Influence: the Psychology of Persuasion*. New York: Quill/William Morrow.

Citizenship and Immigration Canada. Minister of Public Works and Government Services Canada. 2000. *Welcome to Canada: What You Should Know*. http://www.cic.gc.ca/english/newcomer/welcome/wel-10e.html (04/15/2004).

Clarke, Sarah. 2001. "DisABILITY in the Classroom: The Forgotten Dimension of Diversity? In Janice Newton *et al* (Eds). *Voices from the Classroom: Reflections on Teaching and Learning in Higher Education*. Aurora, Ontario: Garamond Press.

Clarkson, Adrienne. July 1, 2001. An immigrant's progress. *Maclean's*, 114.27, 26.

Clarkson, Austin. 2001. "Teaching Styles/Learning Styles: The Myers Briggs Model." In Janice Newton *et al* (Eds.*). Voices from the Classroom: Reflections on Teaching and Learning in Higher Education.* Aurora, Ontario: Garamond Press.

Cortina, Joe, Janet Elder and Katherine Connet. 1996. *Comprehending College Textbooks: Steps to understanding and remembering what you read,* Third Edition. New York: The McGraw-Hill Companies, Inc.

"Cost of Underemployed Immigrants to Canada's Economy Quantified." May/June 2002. *Population Today.* http://www.prb.org/pdf/PT_mayjun02.pdf

Davies, Scott and Neil Guppy. 1998. "Race in Canadian Education". In Vic Satzewich (ed.). *Racism and Social Inequality in Canada.* Toronto: TEP.

Dei, George. 1996. *Anti-Racism Education. Theory and Practice,* Halifax: Fernwood Publishing.

Driver, Deanna. Mar 4, 2003. 'Peace of mind is priceless,' say MDs new to Canada: higher taxes and lower pay are worth the tradeoff for two Nigerian physicians who left the 'hostile' environment of practicing in the U.S. for Regina. *Medical Post,* 39.9, 49.

Dyer, Gwynne. Jan/Feb 2001. Visible Majorities. *Canadian Geographic,* 121.1, 44.

Fleras, Augie and Jean Elliott. 2002. *Engaging Diversity: Multiculturalism in Canada. Toronto*: Nelson Canada.

Floyd, Richard. 1995. *Success in the Social Sciences: Writing and research for Canadian Students.* Toronto: Harcourt Brace.

Frideres, J. 2002. Immigrants, Integration and the Intersection of Identities. www.canada.metropolis.net/events/Diversity/Immigration.pdf (15/04/2004).

Giarrusso, Roseann, Judith Richlin-Klonsky, William G. Roy, and Ellen Strenski. 1994. *A Guide to Writing Sociology Papers.* New York: St. Martin's Press.

Ginsburg, Jerry. 2001a. "The Gregorc Model of Learning Styles." In Janice Newton *et al* (Eds.*). Voices from the Classroom: Reflections on Teaching and Learning in Higher Education.* Aurora, Ontario: Garamond Press.

Ginsburg, Jerry. 2001b. "The Dialectic of Course Development: I Theorize, They React...Then? In Janice Newton *et al* (Eds.*)*. *Voices from the Classroom: Reflections on Teaching and Learning in Higher Education.* Aurora, Ontario: Garamond Press.

Goar, Carol. Apr 14, 2004. We cannot let immigrants fail. *Toronto Star* [ONT Edition], A22.

Goodwin, Marta. Jul 6, 2003. Canadians can learn a lot from newcomers. *Vancouver Courier*, p.11.

Granatstein, JL & Rawlinson, H. Graham. Jul 1, 2001. Canada's brain gain: the nation's story is one of people coming, leaving and returning. *Maclean's*, 114.27, 22.

Griffiths, Rudyard. April 29, 2002. Open the gates wide. *Maclean's*, 115.17, 28.

Hoodfar, H. 1997. "Feminist Anthropology and Critical Pedagogy: The Anthropology of Classrooms' Excluded Voices". In S. deCastell & M. Bryson (eds.) *Radical Intervention, Politics and Difference/s in Educational Praxis.* Albany State: University of New York Press.

Immen, Wallace. Feb. 18, 2004. *Immigrants welcome, roadblocks ahead.* www.globeandmail.com

James, Carl E. 2001. "Diversity in the Classroom: Engagement and Resistance". In Janice Newton *et al* (Eds.*)*. *Voices from the Classroom: Reflections on Teaching and Learning in Higher Education.* Aurora, Ontario: Garamond Press.

Janigan, Mary. Dec 16, 2002. Immigrants: How many is too many? Who should get in? Can we tell them where to live and what to do? *Maclean's*, 115.50, 20-26.

Johnson, JR., William A., Richard P. Rettig, Gregory M. Scott and Stephen M. Garrison. 1998. *The Sociology Student Writer's Manual.* Upper Saddle River, NJ.: Prentice Hall.

Jones, Vernon Clement. July 03, 2001. Minorities' cars get searched more. *Toronto Star* http://www.geocities.com/CapitolHill/CanadaCustomsandRevenueAgency/ cdncustomsc... (14/09/2004).

Jung, Carl. 1971. *Psychological Types.* Princeton: Princeton University Press.

Kalbach, Madeline A. & Kalbach, Warren E. 1999. Becoming Canadian: Problems of an Emerging Identity. *Canadian Ethnic Studies*, 31.2, 1.

Kanchier, Carole. Feb. 7, 2001. Job fairs: the dos and don'ts: Prepare in advance to take advantage of opportunities; [Final edition] *The Ottawa Citizen*, D.13.

Kapel, Claudine & Shepherd, Catherine. Feb. 23, 2004. Four keys to goals and performance. *Canadian HR Reporter*, 17.4, 18.

Karsh, Yousuf. Greatness exposed. http://collections.ic.gc.ca/heirloom_series/ volume4/118-121.htm (14/9/2004)

Kelly, Jennifer. 1998. *Under the Gaze: Learning to Be Black in White Society*, Halifax: Fernwood Publishing.

Kennedy, Gavin. 2000. *Influence*. Essex, UK: Pearson.

Keung, Nicholas. Mar 25, 2004. Humble man finally finds path to success. *Toronto Star*, B.05.

Kirk, Janis Foord. Apr. 4, 1992. Be prepared: Cardinal rule for all kinds of job interviews. *The Ottawa Citizen*, J.1.

Longitudinal Survey of Immigrants to Canada 2001: Labour market entry Sept 4, 2003 *The Daily* http://www.statcan.ca/english/freepub/89-611-XIE/labour.htm (15/04/2004) http://toronto.cbc.ca/...(14/9/2004).

Markusoff, Jason. May 28, 2003. Path to employment tough walk for immigrants: New centre helps show them the way. *Edmonton Journal*, B.6.

McConaghy, Tom. Feb 95. Multicultural policy under attack. *Phi Delta Kappan*, 76.6, 498.

McGuinty government helping immigrants work in their chosen trade or profession. Feb 20, 2004. http://ogov.newswire.ca/ontario/GPOE/2004/...(15/04/2004).

Moore, Brooke Noel and Richard Parker. 1995. *Critical Thinking*, Fourth Edition. Toronto: Mayfield Publishing Company.

Northey, Margot and Lorne Tepperman. 1986/1993. *Making Sense in the Social Sciences: A Student's Guide to Research, Writing, and Style.* Toronto: Oxford University Press.

Nurse, Donna Bailey. Aug 11, 2003. PW interview with Austin Clarke: A Barbadian abroad. *Publishers Weekly*, 250.32, 250.

O'Day, Danton H. 1991. *How to Succeed at College: The Complete Student Guide.* Oakville: Trilobyte Press.

Peterson, Oscar; Croll, David; Newman, Peter C.; Fraser, John, *et al.* Jan 1, 2000. Forging a new country: they came from all over the globe. *Maclean's*, 112-113.52/1, 172.

Robin, Raizel & Bogomolny, Laura. March 29, 2004. *A competitive edge: How minority hiring practices help keep FedEx, Xerox Canada and Call-Net on top. Canadian Business Online.*
http://www.canadianbusiness.com/article.jsp?content=20040329_59149_59149

Satzewich, Vic. January/February 2004. Racism in Canada. Canadian Dimension. http://www.canadiandimension.mb.ca/v38/v38_1vs.htm (26/09/2004).

Schuyler, Lynne. Dec 2001. The Transformation of Daniel Igali: To become world champion, he'd have to start believing in himself.
http://www.readersdigest.ca/mag_archive.html

Siddiqui, Haroon. Sep. 14, 2000. Immigrants should boycott Canada. *Toronto Star,* A.34.

Sinclair, Sonja. May 15, 2000. No ordinary campers: a unique group of Jewish refugee immigrants has contributed greatly to life in Canada. *Maclean's*, 113.20, 24.

Stevens, Kelli. Feb. 2004. Lack of Foreign Credentials Recognition hurts Immigrants and Canadian Economy. http://www.environmental-center.com/articles/ article1413/article1413.htm (15/04/2004).

"Tak Wah Mak." [BrainGain]. Jul 1, 2001. *Maclean's*, 114. 27, 32.

Tips for Goal Setting. Feb. 23, 2004. *Canadian HR Reporter*, 17.4, 18.

Todd, Douglas. Sep 11, 1995. Chinese asked to examine their own habits. *The Vancouver Sun*, A.1.

UNC-CH Writing Centre. 1998-2005. Effective Academic Writing: http://unc.edu/depts/wcweb/ The Argument. University of North Carolina at Chapel Hill.

Virtual U helps immigrants earn degrees before coming to Canada. July 07, 2004. http://www.workopolis.com (15/9/2004).

Vu, Uyen. May 3, 2004. Canada invites foreign workers but neglects them on arrival. *Canadian HR Reporter*, 17.9, 1.

Vu, Uyen. Sep 8. 2003. From executive to entry level. *Canadian HR Reporter*, 16.15, 1.

Waters, Johanna. Autumn 2003. Flexible citizens? Transnationalism and citizenship amongst economic immigrants in Vancouver. *Canadian Geographer*, 47. 3, 219.

Welcome to Canada. 2003. http://www.cic.gc.ca/english/pdf/pub/welcome.pdf

Wheeler, Daniel. 1980. "Learning Styles: A Tool for Faculty Development". *POD Quarterly* 2 (3–4): 164–74.

Wong, Jan. Aug 31, 2002. A country of sales clerks. *The Globe and Mail*, www.globeandmail.com Print Edition, Page   F4.

Wotherspoon, Terry. 2004. "Education". In Lorne Tepperman and James Curtis (eds.). *Sociology: A Canadian Perspective*. Don Mill: Oxford University Press.

Young, Lesley. Apr 19, 1999. Immigrants' job prospects dim. *HR Reporter*, 12.8, 7.

Yousuf Karsh (1908-) and Malak Karsh (1915-) [BrainGain]. Jul 1, 2001. *Maclean's*. 114(27), 29.

INDEX

CPSIA information can be obtained at www.ICGtesting.com
Printed in the USA
LVOW051404021111

253045LV00017BE/6/P

9 781926 585277